WHAT COULD YOU DO
WITH *MORE* MONEY?

PROVISION
FOR THE
VISION

FUNDING YOUR
VISION IS *EASIER*
THAN YOU THINK

TONY RIVERA | DIANNA RIVERA | KEISHA PEARSON

ΛVΛIL

Cover design by Sara Young
Cover photo by Olha Yefimova
Cover author photo by Andrew van Tilborgh

ISBN: 978-1-962401-59-3   1 2 3 4 5 6 7 8 9 10

Printed in the United States of America

WHAT PEOPLE ARE SAYING ABOUT
PROVISION FOR THE VISION

Provision for the Vision is more than just a book; it's a masterfully crafted guide that beautifully captures the epic odyssey of a remarkable team, united by unshakable faith. My first-hand experience of their journey has allowed me to witness its profound influence within their community . . . and far beyond. This book is a treasured resource of inspiration and information, that will ultimately result in a transformation of both thoughts and deed.

—*Dr. Duane White*
Founder of The Bridge Church Denton,
Texas/Beyond These Shore Ministries
Leader of The o2 Network of Churches & Ministries

Provision for the Vision is such a needed book in every leader's library. Any leader worth his or her salt is full of passion and vision. For most leaders, having a vision is not the problem; providing the resources to manifest the vision is the sticking point. Tony, Dianna, and Keisha have masterfully shared in this book the journey they have been on learning how to bring "Provision for the Vision" God had placed in their hearts. This book contains insights, experiences, and wisdom gained over the last nineteen years of faithfully following a God-birthed Vision—starting with nothing but a burning call and desire to make a difference to this moment where thousands of lives have been impacted and millions of dollars resourced to fund that Vision of making a difference in the lives of precious people. When God put on our hearts to start a school, it was

Tony, Dianna, and Keisha whom I contacted to tap into those insights, experiences, and wisdom they had gained on their journey. We are in our first year at Kingdom Culture Academy and we are thriving!! *Provision for the Vision* could very well be the catalyst that propels you into your season of thriving, not just surviving!!

—*Pastor Lonnie Johns*
Living the Dream
Christ Central/Kingdom Culture Academy/
Renewed Outreach Center

As I read this book, my first thought was—"*. . . where were you years ago?*" I have no doubt that the same thought will be yours as well. The good news is that it is now in your hands. Biblical. User friendly. Pragmatic. Systematic. Affirming. Encouraging. My friends Tony Rivera, Dianna Rivera, and Keisha Pearson have poured their life's work into *Provision for the Vision: Funding Your Vision is Easier Than You Think.* You will not only fund your vision through this resource but will also share it with all other fellow pilgrims.

—*Sam Chand*
Leadership Consultant and Author

There is no greater thrill for a teacher than when the student(s) exceed them! This book combines story-telling and biblical wisdom with practical advice and sequential steps for success with grant funding for community outreach. Every church and non-profit ministry should get ahold of this book and take their advice.

—*Yvonne Sawyer*
President, Hope for Miami

In this remarkable book, my brother Tony, alongside his wife Dianna Rivera and Keisha Pearson, shares a story that is both authentic and deeply inspiring. Having had the privilege of witnessing their journey firsthand over the past nineteen years, I can attest to the extraordinary transformation they have facilitated in their community and beyond. From humble beginnings, they cultivated a ministry that today is both resource-rich and impactful. Their commitment to integrity is unwavering, as evidenced by their consistent success in rigorous financial audits.

The depth of their connection and unwavering commitment to the community is profoundly personal and moving. Seeing the way my brother and Dianna serve with such heartfelt dedication, I am reminded time and again of their immense capacity for compassion. Every soul they meet, without exception, is embraced with such warmth and esteem that it's clear they are seen and cherished as invaluable.

Through nineteen years of tireless dedication to grant writing, they, together, have honed a rare expertise that truly sets them apart. Their ability to guide and mentor promising ministries is unparalleled. What moves me most is their innate skill for nurturing connections that cross any divide, touching lives in deeply personal ways.

—*Raul Rivera*
Founder StartCHURCH

I've had the privilege of watching everything written in this book unfold for the last twenty years. It all really happened! Tony Rivera Jr. has lived the message, principles, and practices of this book for two decades in the inner city of Miami. He is a proven practitioner with a God-given gift to not just do what seems impossible, but also the ability to teach and impart the principles and best practices necessary to accomplish the impossible. What you hold in your hand is a story of God's amazing provision in the most unlikely place and in the most unlikely ways, but it's more than a story. This book is also a playbook, that if taken seriously and followed will help you discover the transformational God possibilities and provision for the vision God has given you within the context He has placed you in. Don't just read the book and follow the principles; catch the heart and the spirit behind the principles.

—*Trey Jones*
Healthy, Growing, Multiplying Churches (HGM), Director

CONTENTS

ACKNOWLEDGMENTS

As we hold this book in our hands, a journey of faith, hope, and relentless dedication, we are deeply aware that such a project is never a solitary endeavor. It is with immense gratitude and profound respect that we acknowledge those who have been instrumental in the journey of writing "Provision for the Vision."

First and foremost, our love and gratitude to the late Bishop Tony Miller and Pastor Kathy Miller, our spiritual parents, who instilled in us the value of relationships and connections and taught us that big doors swing on little hinges. Your encouragement to dream big has been a guiding light, reminding us that there is always a way.

We are forever grateful to Ken and Lisa Albin, who opened the door to Miami for us, setting the stage for this incredible journey.

To Ron and Hope Carpenter and the Redemption Church family, words cannot express our gratitude. Without your pivotal role, we (Tony and Dianna) wouldn't have met Keisha, and this vision would not have come to fruition.

A special acknowledgment to Pastors Robert and the late Rosetta Gray, my (Keisha) mentors, for your wisdom and guidance and for saying "GO!" to the move to Miami.

To the congregations and leadership of Miami Harvest Church/Impact Church, especially Pastors Manny and Victoria, thank you for partnering with us in those formative years and helping lay the foundation of our mission.

To New Harvest Church, where we (Tony and Dianna) had our formative years of early ministry . . . we will always cherish our years in Clewiston; we are a product of your soil, and to Pastors Chuck and Karen Pelham who now pastor there for being lifelong friends and family.

Our sincere appreciation goes to Life Church, where Pastors Ryan and Jennifer, along with Pastors Jody and CJ, gave supernaturally to help launch our church. Your generosity provided the means to complete the renovations; you left an indelible mark on our hearts and ministry.

Duane White, your consistent support as a monthly partner in the first year was a source of strength for us. We are deeply indebted to Joe Correy, Thomas Muthee, Vaughn McLaughlin, and Junior Tucker, whose impact in our first year has been nothing short of transformative.

Our journey would not have been the same without our parents and families: Tony and Rosa Rivera (Tony), Ben and Elma Williams (Dianna), Doretha and Joshua Thompson (Keisha). Your unwavering support and love have been our bedrock.

A special heartfelt mention of gratitude to my (Keisha) aunts and uncles, who are all like parents, for providing a solid foundation for me to launch out.

There is special grace that the Lord gives to children whose parents are called to ministry! To our (Tony and Dianna) daughter, Makenzie Annaliese Rivera, thank you for going on this wild ride! Love you! To my (Keisha) children, Legacy and Legend, you are my greatest gifts and inspiration.

To Rick and Yvonne Sawyer, thank you for opening us to the world of grant funding and mentoring us in navigating these new waters. Your friendship and expertise have been and still are indispensable.

Ero Torrales and Jorge Torrales from the Elite Innovative Family, your support in managing our finances has been paramount.

Alejandro Perez, your wisdom and input have opened new possibilities for us, and we are deeply thankful. Dr. Whye, your access to the school and staff has been crucial in expanding our reach and impact.

To all our clients and partners, your success is our honor! Your trust and collaboration have been pivotal in realizing our shared goals.

To Natasha White, Andrea Jolly, Stephanie McNeil, Baby and Chad Pelham, and Debra Oliva, who believed in the vision of Citi Church when it was just a seedling, your faith and commitment have been a driving force in reaching our community.

Hermana Ester, as our first church member, your place in this journey is so special.

Jennifer Coronel, your faith in our emerging programs and wild snacks has been a source of encouragement and laughter.

Our Citi Church Family at large, your time, investments, contributions, and support have been the lifeblood of our church. We carry each of you in our hearts. To Jorge and Maria Vasquez, Gil and Paula Chaidez, Lilia Altamirano and

Yolanda Lundy—thank you for being pillars. Your reward will be great! . . . Much love to 305!

Dr. Sam Chand, your wisdom has been a guiding light not only in the first few years but even now, twenty years later. Your influence cannot be overstated.

To the AVAIL Team, thank you for your invaluable help in bringing this book project to success. Your expertise and support have been instrumental.

Most importantly, we thank our Lord and Savior Jesus Christ, the cornerstone of our faith and the true source of our vision. This journey is first and foremost a testament to His grace, mercy, and unfailing love.

In conclusion, this book and our journey are a tapestry woven from the contributions of each one of you. We stand today because of your faith, support, and love. For this, we are eternally grateful.

—Tony Rivera, Dianna Rivera, and Keisha Pearson

A WORD FROM THE AUTHORS

The three of us are a team. We've traveled the road of faith, hope, and love together as we planted Citi Church in Miami and nurtured its growth. Throughout the book, we speak most often with one voice, so we use "we". Occasionally when one of us tells a personal story or shares a specific insight, we'll identify who is speaking.

CHAPTER 1

OPEN EYES, OPEN HEARTS

My instant reaction was, *Oh Lord, no! This won't work at all!*

TONY

Dianna and I had just stepped into an abandoned building that a pastor recommended for our new church plant. It was awful beyond words. That moment reminds me of a similar response from Ezekiel only a few years after the Babylonians invaded Israel and took many of the people into exile.

"The Lord took hold of me, and I was carried away by the Spirit of the Lord to a valley filled with bones. He led me all around among the bones that covered the valley floor. They were scattered everywhere across the ground and were completely dried out. Then he asked me, 'Son of man, can these bones become living people again?'" (see Ezekiel 37:1-3)

I felt God was asking me a similar question: "Tony, can this wreck of a building become a source of light and life for the people of this community in Miami?"

Like Ezekiel, I would have shaken my head and responded, "O Sovereign Lord, you alone know the answer to that."

God's instructions to Ezekiel resonated in my heart:

Then he said to me, "Speak a prophetic message to these bones and say, 'Dry bones, listen to the word of the Lord! This is what the Sovereign Lord says: Look! I am going to put breath into you and make you live again! I will put flesh and muscles on you and cover you with skin. I will put breath into you, and you will come to life. Then you will know that I am the Lord.'"—vv. 4-6

It would take a while, but eventually, God blessed our efforts, just as God blessed Ezekiel's obedience:

So, I spoke this message, just as he told me. Suddenly as I spoke, there was a rattling noise all across the valley. The bones of each body came together and attached themselves as complete skeletons. Then as I watched, muscles and flesh formed over the bones. Then skin formed to cover their bodies, but they still had no breath in them. —vv. 7-8

Let me back up and explain how we arrived at the building that day. In the spring of 2004, Dianna and I were serving at Destiny World Outreach, leading Destiny Bible College, and Keisha was serving in a thriving church, Redemption World Outreach Center, in Greenville, South Carolina. We loved it there. I was teaching young leaders the principles of church planting, and one day, I sensed God tap me on the shoulder and whisper, "Now it's your turn to do what you've been helping others do." A pastor in Miami heard that we were interested in planting a church in the city, and he contacted me with an offer to show us a building.

When we arrived, he took us to a Cracker Barrel in an affluent community north of Miami, and then he drove us the thirty miles or so to the building. Along the way, the landscape changed—no, not rivers and mountains, but the houses, apartments, streets, shops, and restaurants. It was like we were driving from an affluent American suburb to a disadvantaged community in a foreign land. And this assessment was almost literally true because many of the people in that part of Miami are new immigrants from Central and South America, and many are undocumented. On the way, the pastor told us that no one had been willing to plant a church in that part of the city because there were so few resources, and the people didn't trust those from the outside. (I wanted to say, "Well, thanks a lot! You could have dropped that little bit of information on me while we were in South Carolina!")

We drove through the neighborhood and finally parked next to an abandoned building. "We're here," the pastor cheerily remarked. It had been abandoned for about fifteen years, but it wasn't unoccupied. Homeless people and addicts had sheltered there and let me say delicately that sanitation wasn't high on their priority list. Weeds and bushes were growing from the sidewalks, and most of the windows were broken out. It wasn't a good first impression.

We got out of the pastor's car, and he unlocked the doors. When we stepped inside, the smell of recent inhabitants and the damp, moldy odor of years of storms pouring rain through the windows was shocking. Termites had eaten parts of the structure. I walked onto what used to be a platform, but I had to be careful because the wood was rotten. That's when I thought, *No way, Lord!* But at that moment, God gave me a vision of hundreds of people in that room praising Him— people of different colors, different races, and different languages. The vision sealed the deal. The hope of having that kind of impact in the neighborhood was a more powerful force in my heart than all my fears . . . but only for an instant. Suddenly, it seemed utterly impossible that this wreck of a building could become an outpost of God's kingdom. We walked out, and the pastor put chains and a lock on the doors.

After only a few steps, an elderly lady came running across the street. She yelled in Spanish, "Eres el pastor!" ("You are the pastor!").

I quickly responded, "No, I'm not the pastor here."

She looked dejected and mumbled, "Yo he estado orando por tres meses que las puertas de esta iglesia se abren yo pensaba que tú eras el pastor." ("I have been praying for three months that the doors of this church would open. I thought you were the pastor.")

Immediately, she walked away back across the street.

When we got in the car, Dianna gave me "that look." I knew exactly what she was thinking: *How could you say we're not going to plant a church here?* It was a long ride back to the Cracker Barrel, but Dianna and I were soon convinced that God had called us to plant a church . . . in that building . . . in Allapattah.

God was opening our eyes to the desperate needs in the neighborhood, and He was preparing our hearts to embrace the people there.

Six months later, we took possession of the property. In October, to be near the reconstruction, Dianna and I and our young daughter, Makenzie, moved into a house next door. We sometimes heard gunshots, and one day Child Protective Services arrived at a house down the street because the mother had been pimping her teenage daughter. For weeks, we had noticed that different men went in and out of the house every night—now we knew why. That part of Miami has big problems with crime, drugs, and violence. It has the highest juvenile delinquency rate in the state. Facilities—schools, healthcare, police, the fire department, and all the rest—had been overlooked as the rest of the city grew. After CPS took the young girl away, Dianna looked at me and asked, "What have you gotten us into?" It was a very good question. God was opening our eyes to the desperate needs in the neighborhood, and He was preparing our hearts to embrace the people there.

It wasn't easy. When we weren't working on the building, we took prayer walks. On the first one, we knocked on doors to meet our neighbors, but most people wouldn't come out to meet us, let alone invite us in. Almost everyone was suspicious because we were outsiders, and they were wary of US Immigration and Customs Enforcement (ICE) agents who might arrest and deport them. I didn't think we looked like law enforcement, especially wearing our Citi Church shirts, but fear is a powerful force. Another factor is that Jehovah's Witnesses regularly canvas the area, and I'm sure some of the people assumed we were with them.

But a few people were willing to talk with us. When we asked them to tell us what they hoped for and what they needed, many of them talked about the lack of services for children and teenagers. Schools weren't safe, and the streets were dangerous. With nothing to do, kids gravitated to gangs and other self-destructive behaviors. These conversations went a long way to crystallize our vision to provide services for kids and, by extension, their families.

Our grand opening was May 21, 2005. We'd handed out flyers all over the community, and we invited everyone who would talk to us. That day, 300 people worshipped God in our freshly renovated building! The vision had become a reality. Many of those who came flew in from all over the country to celebrate with us. It was a wonderful start, but the next week, only ten people showed up . . . and five of us were on the staff team! I went from the high of exaltation to the low of deep discouragement. Still, we believed God would give us favor—somehow, someday.

The morning of our second service, I realized the work had only begun. Two months later, we brought people from the Salvation Army's homeless shelter to our church services. I preached with passion on "Being Awakened to the God of Possibilities," but when I looked at the people sitting on the front row, they were all sound asleep. I felt more than discouraged; I was depressed. After the service, I told Dianna to leave without me. I needed to stay for a while to pray. I went to the altar and prayed, "Lord, I'm so angry! I followed you to come here. I made decisions that changed the trajectory of my life, but this is a failure. I just can't do this!"

I knew He was asking me to surrender my vision of success and let Him do what only He can do—in His way, in His timing, with His resources, to care for the people He loves.

I sensed God whisper, "I know you can't, but I can." I knew He was asking me to surrender my vision of success and let Him do what only He can do—in His way, in His timing, with His resources, to care for the people He loves. This was a pivotal moment for me.

We met Yvonne Sawyer in early 2006, the founding director of Family & Children Faith Coalition (now known as Hope for Miami) who would eventually open the world of grant funding to us. Yvonne came to Miami from New York City to marry Rick Sawyer in 1998. She had been on the staff of Redeemer Presbyterian Church—which was planted by the late Rev. Dr. Tim Keller. (She was the first person he hired in January of 1990.) In 1991, inspired by Tim's *Ministries of Mercy*[1] book and his vision for city transformation, she began forming the non-profit community ministry Hope for New York. She was the first Executive Director (1992). From then on, until she left to marry Rick in October 1998–she raised funds, recruited volunteers, started new 501(c)(3) ministries, etc.—learning the skills that she needed for the founding of Hope for Miami. Yvonne asked if we'd be interested in organizing a summer camp for kids from 8:00 each morning until 6:00 in the evening. It was being funded through a government grant program she had enlisted. We thought it was a good fit for us, but a few days later, she called to say that a church with a good track record of hosting these summer camps had agreed to host one that summer, so she had to withdraw her invitation. However, only days later, she called back to say that the other church had backed out. "Are you still interested?" she asked.

I said, "Yes! We sure are!" but we had only a week to hire staff, prepare facilities, secure the curriculum, and recruit thirty-six kids to sign up for our program.

---

1   Tim Keller, *Ministries of Mercy: The Call of the Jericho Road* (Phillipsburg, NJ: P & R Publishing, 1997).

Yvonne appreciated how we ran our camp, and she began to cultivate a relationship with us. We had been operating under the auspices of her organization, but she suggested we apply for our own grants and become independent. She encouraged us to apply for a "starter grant" of $25,000, and when it was accepted, we used the money to create a class on English as a second language and started a computer lab at the church. We planned to help people, mostly the parents of the kids we tutored, become computer literate so they could communicate more effectively with family, friends, agencies, and organizations throughout the city. The first person to sit at a computer was Hermana Ester, a seventy-year-old lady from Honduras who had never sat in front of a computer. When she finished the course, she sent her first email . . . to me. What a joy!

We asked God to lead us to a strategy for the next generation, and He led us to adopt a school in the neighborhood, Comstock Elementary, a struggling school with a new principal, Alejandro Perez. The week before school started, we asked the principal if we could provide breakfast for the teachers, administrators, and staff members. He was glad for us to be involved. That morning, we decorated tables with tablecloths and flowers, and we laid out a wonderful buffet. The teachers and staff members were both astonished and grateful. Several commented that no one had ever done anything like that for them. We were operating on a shoestring budget and we had very little money left after paying for the breakfast, but we donated $200 to the school library for new books. The librarian was so moved that he began to cry. He told us, "I've been a librarian for twenty-five years, and this is the first donation we've ever received." The principal became a friend and partner in our efforts to have an impact on kids, teachers, parents, and everyone else connected to the school.

In a short time, our personal funds were running on fumes, so I planned to get a job teaching. I had taught in junior high earlier in my career, so I was sure this was going to be an easy transition. One morning in early 2006, I was standing in line at Starbucks and overheard a job interview at a table nearby. A woman was applying for a job with an organization that tutors kids. I even heard them talk about the hourly pay. This was a much better option than full-time teaching. I could lead the church and make extra money part-time. Later, I told the Comstock principal, Alejandro Perez, my plan, and to my surprise, he instantly remarked, "Don't do it!" He explained that the tutoring program was begun in response to President George W. Bush's educational initiative, No Child Left Behind. Instead of me working personally for the program, he suggested we could apply to be one of the tutoring providers, with several tutors and many students. This would make our church a hub of the community and multiply our connections with kids and their parents.

Typically, a startup church isn't a good candidate to become a site for tutoring, but we spent days working late into the night on our application, and we were approved by the state of Florida. I quickly realized that was only part of the process: We had to also apply to the school district to receive kids who needed tutoring services. We worked like crazy to write another proposal, and again, we were approved. Mr.

Perez was a terrific ally during this process, and we launched our little tutoring program. Within two years, the Lord blessed us: We grew to have seven locations in three states.

On October 15, 2005, Hurricane Wilma whipped through Miami. It was the most powerful storm ever recorded in the Atlantic, a Category 5 with sustained winds at 150 mph and gusts up to 183 mph. Our neighborhood was devastated—we suffered catastrophic damage, loss of power, low fuel supplies, and a shortage of food and water. The power was out in the entire neighborhood except for the elderly living facilities and Citi Church. A miracle! We gathered our Citi Church team together and went house to house, checking on people and providing sandwiches and water. This proved to be one of the best messages we could communicate to our community: "We love you, and we're here for you."

Those early years of Citi Church showed us that we needed to depend on God for, well, everything. People were suspicious of us, so we had to earn their trust; we needed a clear and workable strategy, and God led us to focus on kids and their families; we didn't have financial resources, but God led us to Yvonne Sawyer, who graciously taught us how to secure grants so our ministries could expand and touch the lives of people God had led us to love and serve. As I've shared this story with pastors and leaders across the country, I've told them that we learned to secure grants out of necessity to keep our doors open, but every church, large or small, in a wealthy area or a poor one, can always use more resources to expand God's kingdom. If we can do it, you can do it.

DIANNA

When our friends invited us to Miami to show us a building we might use to plant a church, they first took us to a restaurant in Ft. Lauderdale. The neighborhood had lovely homes on beautiful streets. I could imagine planting a church in a neighborhood like that! But then they drove us to the inner city of Miami. They hadn't told us anything about the building, which was wise because we wouldn't have gone there. We drove down on the 112 and got off on 22nd Avenue. The neighborhood didn't look at all like the one in Ft. Lauderdale. Still, I was keeping an open mind. I was excited about planting a church . . . somewhere . . . anywhere, and if this was where God was leading us, I was for it. When we parked in front of the building, I think God let me look beyond its decrepit condition, at least until I walked through the doors. At that moment, something in me jumped, like a baby kicking its mother.

All of us took our time walking and inspecting the interior of the building. I didn't say much. I was trying to take it all in. When we left out of the side entrance, I saw the woman running toward us, yelling, "Pastor! Pastor!" I felt her presence was prophetic—surely, this was one of God's confirmations. But when she asked Tony if he was going to start a church there, he instantly told her, "No." I knew that's how he felt after walking through the building, but I believed God was in it. (As a strange sequel to the story, as we walked to the car, I turned to see the lady cross the street back to her home, but I didn't see her. We never saw her again. Maybe God sent her just to test us, or maybe she was an angel on a mission.)

The work of renovation lasted from July 2004 until our grand opening in May the following year. We were planting a church—not in a thriving, growing, affluent community where we could count on resources of volunteers and generous offerings, but in an area where people had very little and often closed their doors in our faces. Still, we sensed God's clear calling to that community. We had to start small. We heard and read about other church plants that were booming, but the only booms we heard were gunshots. We decided not to despise these days of small beginnings. the late Bishop Tony Miller, our pastor and spiritual father, would always say, "Big doors swing on little hinges," which are individual points of connection with people God puts in our path. God brought the new principal to Comstock Elementary, Alejandro Perez, and he opened his arms to a partnership with us. God brought Yvonne Sawyer to partner with us to launch a summer camp, and the friendship blossomed so that she taught us how to raise grant money. We put our toe in the water with a starter grant, and the Lord blessed us with the funds to create a computer lab and teach people to speak and write in English. There were many small, seemingly insignificant turning points when God provided and led us in a decision, and we were able to take the next step to advance His kingdom in our neighborhood in Miami.

When we were down, we picked each other up with a fresh shot of faith in God's sovereignty, love, and power.

We had some guest preachers at Citi Church from time to time, including our friend, Duane White, Founding Pastor of The Bridge Church in Denton, Texas and Leader of the O2 Network of Churches. His message was simple and profound: "One by one by one by one." God was calling us to do the next thing, to have the next conversation, to pray the next prayer, to make the next call. Elisabeth Elliot was the wife of Jim Elliot, one of the men who was martyred by the Auca Indians in Peru, as described in her book, *Through Gates of Splendor.* Her loss drove her deeper into the arms of God, and one of the lessons she learned and taught countless others was simply to "do the next thing." She wrote:

> *Have you had the experience of feeling as if you've got far too many burdens to bear, far too many people to take care of, and far too many things on your list to do? You just can't possibly do it, and you get in a panic, and you just want to sit down and collapse in a pile and feel sorry for yourself.*
>
> *Well, I've felt that way a good many times in my life, and I go back over and over again to an old Saxon legend, which I'm told is carved in an old*

English parson somewhere by the sea. I don't know where this is. But this is a poem which was written about that legend. The legend is "Do the next thing." And it's spelled in what I suppose is Saxon spelling. "D-O-E" for "do," "the," and then next, "N-E-X-T." "Thing"-"T-H-Y-N-G-E."[2]

"One by one" became our guiding slogan. Small steps took us a long way. Oh, we had our moments of discouragement. When we were down, we picked each other up with a fresh shot of faith in God's sovereignty, love, and power.

KEISHA

When I was an engineering student at Clemson University, I participated in a School of Ministry associated with Redemption World Outreach Center. During that time, Pastor Tony was leading Destiny Bible College, and it was so effective that our pastor closed our School of Ministry so we could join Destiny Bible College. I was on a career path in electrical engineering, and when I met Pastors Tony and Dianna, I was involved in a leadership development program with General Electric, with a job almost guaranteed with the company. I really enjoyed and appreciated Pastors Tony and Dianna, so when they invited me to travel with them on a weekend trip to Miami, I thought, *Hey, I'm a college student. A weekend in Miami? Why not?* I had no idea they were thinking about planting a church down there. I was going for a fun vacation. While we were there, I spent some time with Pastor Tony's

---

2 Cited by Marci Ferrell, "Do the Next Thing" (A Reminder from Elisabeth Elliot)", Thankful Homemaker, https://thankfulhomemaker.com/do-the-next-thing/.

brother, Pastor Manny Rivera, who was leading a church in a different part of the city. He asked, "So, you're moving to Miami to help plant a church?"

I responded, "Nope. I'm just here for a free trip to hang out for a few days."

He laughed and told me, "I think God is leading you to Miami."

I didn't miss a beat: "No chance. I already have a career plan, and it doesn't include Miami." (When people ask why I went with them, I say, "They tricked me!" That's not really true . . . but it's not completely false either. They somehow failed to tell me *everything* about the trip.)

You can probably imagine the conversations on the drive back to South Carolina. Here I am thinking, *I came for a free trip, and they're making plans to move to Miami to start a church—a church that I didn't know anything about!* Pastor Tony and Dianna were wrestling with God's leading to plant a church—in the disaster of a building they had walked through—even though Dianna had a prophetic sense God was leading them there. I heard them talking, but much of the time, I wasn't listening. I was doing my own wrestling with God. Why had He let me come on this trip? So much for a "free trip." How could I turn my back on the years of hard work to get an engineering degree? How could I say no to a terrific job opportunity with one of the premier companies in the country? But then, how could I say "no" to God if He wanted me in Miami with Pastors Tony and Dianna?

I still have a journal of my musings with God that spring. I studied the Scriptures and asked God to give me clear direction. Gideon became my hero and model for gaining clarity from the Lord. I told God that if He wanted me to join them in Miami, He'd have to do several specific things to open doors, close doors, provide resources, and give me a clear sense of His leading. One by one, He fulfilled all my requests, so I finished my classwork, walked at graduation in May, finished my internship, and moved to Miami in August.

Instantly, I experienced culture shock. I'm not sure what it's like to move to Outer Mongolia, but I'm pretty sure it's something like a South Carolina girl moving into the 'hood in inner-city Miami. People there didn't look like me, talk like me, think like me, or wave and be friendly like me. I questioned if Miami was even part of the United States! On the drive down, I was full of faith . . . but the day after I arrived, I wondered if I'd lost my mind. Pastors Tony and Dianna were finalizing things back in South Carolina, so I was there by myself. I was in the city for two months before they showed up.

Fast forward about a year. One of the first events we held after our first service in the renovated building was hosting a movie night for kids and their families. We drove to every part of the community and knocked on doors to invite people to come. For some reason, they were far more receptive to this invitation to leave their homes and come to us than they were to open their doors when we went to them. Many of the parents let their children go back to the church with us—no releases to be signed, no asking for our cell numbers, nothing. Our only credentials were the Citi Church shirts we were wearing. Each of our cars felt like we had about twenty kids packed inside! We showed an animated Pixar movie and served popcorn and drinks. It was 10:00 p.m. when it was over, and we took the kids back to the homes where we had picked them up. None of the parents complained that we were bringing their children back so late. A number of them asked, "When are you doing this again?"

This was a revelation to us. God had given us a key to unlock doors that had been shut in our faces over and over again. Kids love movies, and because we're with a church, their parents trusted us implicitly. (That's right. The parents didn't trust us enough to talk to us, but they trusted us with the care and protection of their children.)

A few parents came along with their kids that night, including a single mom, Yolanda Lundy, and her three children. She started bringing them to our services, and today, almost two decades later, they're still members, and she is a faithful volunteer in our nursery. Her son is in the Air Force in the Middle East, one daughter is in college, and the other daughter has a dream to become a flight attendant.

Movie night went so well that we planned "Game Night" so parents could play board games with their children. Many of the parents had never played a board game in their lives. They loved it! When they left, we gave each family one of the games so they could play at home. Again, God used these simple events to give us meaningful connections with people in our neighborhood.

I had been looking forward to a rewarding and lucrative career in engineering, but God took me on a detour. Now, I'm an engineer for the kingdom. My work at Citi Church has been far more rewarding, and if blessings are the currency of heaven, far more lucrative than anything I could have imagined.

My promise to you is that if you're faithful in the small things, God will multiply your impact.

SMALL BEGINNINGS

I (Tony) remember a conversation with the principal of Comstock Elementary, Mr. Perez. He said, "Pastor, the companies that move into our neighborhood come and go, but the key to your success is that you stay. Your presence—your love and the way you serve people—is what sets your church apart." And in that moment, I decided that Citi Church would be a church that "stayed."

My promise to you is that if you're faithful in the small things, God will multiply your impact. If God can work through us in this part of Miami, he can certainly work through you in your community. God spoke through the prophet Zechariah, "It is not by force nor by strength, but by my Spirit, says the Lord of Heaven's Armies" (4:6). This means we have to give up on trusting in our talents and resources. Oh, it's wonderful that we have them, but trouble comes when we rely on them instead of God. When we trust him, he marshals "Heaven's Armies" to fight for us.

I've never met a pastor or leader who said, "We don't need more resources to accomplish what God has put on our hearts. We're good." No, a God-inspired vision always exceeds our existing resources, so we need to trust God to give us creative ways to fill our hands so we can open our hands to the people He has called us to love. This book is about the convergence of two things: vision and resources. God has led us to tap into sources of funding we had no idea existed, but when we found them, we saw God provide in super-abundance . . . and He's providing even more all the time.

Isn't that what your heart longs for? Don't you want to see God "accomplish infinitely more than we might ask or think"? When He does, we'll worship like Paul in his prayer for the Ephesians, "Glory to Him in the church and in Christ Jesus through all generations forever and ever! Amen" (3:20-21).

At the end of each chapter, you'll find some questions to help you reflect on what you've read and to stimulate discussion with your team, class, or group. Don't rush through these. It's not a timed drill! Take your time, think and pray, and trust God to give you His heart and His strategies.

THINK ABOUT IT:

1) Has God ever led you to do something you thought was, well, crazy? If so, how did you respond?

2) What part of the story of planting Citi Church inspires you? What part baffles you?

3) Do you agree or disagree with the statement: "A God-inspired vision always exceeds our existing resources"? Explain your answer.

4) Why is it important to come to an end of trusting in our talents and resources? How can we know we're there . . . or not?

5) What do you hope to get out of this book?

CHAPTER 2

SHATTERING COMMON MYTHS

When we shared our grant funding strategy with a pastor and his team, he immediately rejected the idea. "We're not going to let the government tell us what to do!" he insisted. "They can't stop us from preaching the gospel. That's who we are, and that's not going to change!" He wasn't finished. Before we could address his concerns, he told us, "I don't want the government nosying around in our finances. If we get a grant, they'll control us."

Other pastors have visited our church to see how our programs are integrated into the community and are having a significant impact on schools, kids, and parents. They ask, "How do you do that?" When we explain that most of this is funded through grants from the local, state, and federal government, they shake their heads and instantly write us off: "Oh, we can't do that. It's too much work, and we can't spare the manpower." When many of those same pastors came to see us a year or so later and witnessed how our reach into the community had expanded and deepened through grant-funded programs, they still insisted it wasn't what they could imagine doing.

We understand the immediate resistance to the concept. Securing grants is new to most people as it was to us, and it doesn't fit quickly and easily into the usual ministry strategies. When we are informed, however, our resistance diminishes. In this chapter, we want to address the most common myths many leaders believe about grant funding.

Myth #1: Churches and Religious Nonprofit Organizations Can't Get Grants

This is a misplaced assumption of availability, not the fear of control. Many church leaders assume the separation of church and state excludes even the possibility of government agencies approving grant requests for them. The fact is that government agencies have funds dedicated to programs for kids, families, schools, and communities, and if a church can show they can provide services that will meet the goals of the agencies, the money is often released. These agencies realize that the church is one of the (if not the) most effective organizations to care for people in the community . . . especially in urban settings. On the other side, many people in inner cities trust churches to care for them more than government agencies.

A website dedicated to informing church leaders about government grants explains:

> *Church grants or more properly, faith-based grants, are available through many foundations and the*

Federal government. There are support programs that offer grants for churches by targeting funding for community-based programs. This category might include after-school programs for at-risk students, early reading programs, classes on safe food preparation, or any other targeted program that affects communities.[3]

If the proposal is compelling and the implementation plan is sound, agencies will often provide funds.

Private foundations like the DeMoss Foundation and the Mustard Seed Foundation have a national reach and could be good resources, but most of the grant funding we've received has come through government agencies. We've observed that private foundations are often fairly restrictive in providing funding—you often have to know someone in the foundation and have an established reputation. But government agencies are far more open to startups like Citi Church in our early days, as well as churches that are just getting their feet wet in writing grant proposals. If the proposal is compelling and the implementation plan is sound, agencies will often provide funds.

---

3 "Church Grants," Government Grant.US, http://governmentgrant.us/church-grants/.

Myth #2: Our Church Is Too Small

We want to laugh at this myth! It would be hard to be smaller than our church on that second Sunday when we had ten people show up. Agencies aren't looking for size; they're looking for competence to administer the program. In fact, some of these agencies only fund organizations with a yearly budget of less than $250,000. (We certainly qualified when we began!)

"Capacity-building grants" are a good way to jump into this kind of funding. Our very first grant was called a "starter grant," and we were awarded $25,000 to set up English classes and a computer lab. At the time we only had an operating budget of $60,000, no paid staff, and a lot of dreams and aspirations.

Small churches—in inner cities, suburbs, and rural areas—can qualify for grants that allow them to provide valuable services for their communities. When we started, we had no idea there were so many avenues to get funding for programs to care for people around us. In fact, we're still uncovering opportunities. The money is there; we just need to craft programs that align with the goals of the agency . . . and that's far easier than you might think.

You may read about enormous grants to large organizations but don't be scared away by the size. You can find plenty of sources to provide $5,000, $10,000, or $20,000 for programs that will give you a stronger reach into your community.

Myth #3: It's Too Hard!

A pastor asked us to come to his church to consult with him about grant funding. His team had many of the usual questions and believed a common myth that "it's too hard." As we sat in the office, Dianna went online and found an agency that had $10,000 available for a program that fits the church's outreach strategy. Together, Dianna, Keisha, and the team filled out the application, and submitted it on the spot! They were approved just weeks later. The grant has been renewed three times so far but at higher levels each time. Too hard? Not so much.

Many pastors assume they have to write proposals that are the length of a John Grisham novel, but most documents are five to twenty pages, and after you've written one, you can cut and paste most of the information for the next ones. All proposals have similar contents: They want to know who you are, the needs you propose to meet, the program and plan, the qualifications of the leader and the team, and past successes. (We'll outline all of the elements in Chapter 9, Nuts and Bolts.) When we started, Yvonne Sawyer mentored us. She believed in us and helped us craft the first proposal. We wrote it, sent it to her for feedback, made the edits, and sent it to her again. Finally, we were ready. It's not that difficult, and besides, we can teach you how to write winning proposals, so your learning curve isn't very steep.

Another aspect of feeling overwhelmed is that the agencies seem huge and distant, like there's a gigantic organization in Washington staffed by aliens. That's just not the case. Many of the connections are in your own neighborhood. City and county agencies have money earmarked for certain types of programs, and they're eager to find worthy partners. We've developed deep roots in Miami to know how the government operates and who holds the purse strings. For instance, about half of the funding for YMCAs comes from government agencies, including the Departments of Justice, Health and Human Services, Housing and Urban Development, Homeland Security, and Veterans Affairs.[4] All of these have local offices to work with organizations like the YMCA and also with churches who have programs that fit their objectives.

Our first tutoring program was a federally funded initiative from the Department of Education. The dollars allocated for No Child Left Behind went to the states. As we mentioned earlier, we applied to the state for funding, and then we applied to the school district to administer the program in our local school system. Similarly, some federal Covid funding was dedicated to housing, which was sent to the states to administer. Local organizations could then tap into those funds to provide housing for people in need. In everything we do, our primary contacts aren't in Washington; they're in our community and likely in yours, too.

Myth #4: Grant Funders Will Control Us!

This is one of the most common misconceptions. Many church leaders don't trust the government, so they assume the worst. Pastors have told us (with supreme confidence) that if they get a grant from a government agency, they'll have to change their statement of faith to be liberal, and the agency will take control of the church. We want to respond, "Look at us. Take a good look at us. We've received dozens of grants, and nothing remotely similar to that has happened."

---

4 "YMCA Federal Funding Overview," https://www.ywca.org/wp-content/uploads/YWCA-Federal-Funding-Overview-Handout-20180215.pdf.

But of course, one of the requirements of those who receive grants is accountability—they want to know we're doing what we said we'd do. If we've agreed to receive money to feed one hundred people each month for a year, the agency wants an accurate and timely report from us. That's good and right and fair, and in fact, they should expect nothing less.

> **People want to know if our actions match our words. If we preach the love of God but seldom touch the lives of people in need, they have every reason to wonder if we mean what we say.**

Some agencies have a requirement that we can't proselytize or share our faith with people in the funded program. We respond to this requirement in two ways: First, we have many ways to let people know we're following Jesus. We wear Citi Church shirts, we talk about our relationship with God, and we often serve people in our church facilities. We're preaching Jesus through our compassion and our service. As Francis of Assisi noted, "Preach the gospel at all times, and if necessary, use words."[5] And second, when we participate in a program, like after-school activities or tutoring, we can speak up about Jesus as soon as the program has ended. To have one more degree of separation, if specific staff members are working in the program until 6:00 p.m., at 6:01, a pastor or other volunteer can ask if anyone wants to know more about how to be forgiven and have a sense of purpose through a relationship with Christ. This isn't dishonest; it honors the commitment and creatively finds ways to share the gospel.

People want to know if our actions match our words. If we preach the love of God but seldom touch the lives of people in need, they have every reason to wonder if we mean what we say. But as we move into the community to meet needs in tangible, meaningful ways, we build trust so that when they hear our message of salvation by grace through faith, they're more willing to listen.

Myth #5: We Don't Know How to Manage a Grant

At Citi Church, we manage programs funded by grants the same way we manage every other department, ministry, or business: We define objectives, plan our activities, recruit a leader and a team, mobilize the necessary resources, and get to work. The only differences are in the source of funding (grants instead of tithes and offerings) and the reporting structure (to the agency in addition to church leaders). If you can lead a successful Vacation Bible School, you can manage programs funded by the government.

---

5   Hanael Bianchi, "Preach the Gospel at all times (and without any exceptions)," Catholic Review, 27 Oct. 2017, https://catholicreview.org/preach-gospel-times-without-exceptions/.

We learned a lot from our partnership with Yvonne Sawyer leading an after-school program. We were thrilled to work under her organization, but when she told us we were ready to go out on our own, we questioned if we were ready. We applied anyway, in spite of our apprehension and fear, and we were awarded our first "large" grant. Our work with Family & Children Faith Coalition showed us that we could pull off a program with excellence, so it wasn't a big jump to manage our own.

Myth #6: Grants Are Only About Dollars

Some agencies, foundations, and companies will give tangible resources but not money. Years ago, we started Citi Christian Academy, and soon, we had sports programs up and running. We often played teams from private schools in much more affluent parts of the city, and our equipment wasn't up to their standards. We applied for a grant from the athletic equipment giant Riddell, and they gave us credit for $10,000 worth of helmets, shoulder pads, and other football equipment. The boys on our team were thrilled to wear top-of-the-line gear on the field.

One year, we wanted to provide food for Thanksgiving for people in our church who didn't have enough to provide a nice meal for their families. We wrote a letter to a local grocery store to share our story and explain the needs of our people. We asked them to donate gift cards so our people could shop there. They gladly gave us twenty-five cards, each for $50.

AmeriCorps is a federal agency that "provides opportunities for Americans of all backgrounds to serve their country, address the nation's most pressing challenges, and improve lives and communities."[6] Those who participate aren't paid a salary, but they receive a monthly stipend to cover a wide range of expenses, including rent. This means a church can apply for a grant to at least partially fund a staff member who is actively involved in serving the community.

Myth #7: Grant Funding Is Free Money

The assumption is the opposite of high control. Some people assume that if they get money from a government agency, they can spend it any way they want. Yes, the funding is incredibly valuable, but it always comes with strings: We have to use it to fulfill the objective described in the proposal. That's not unfair, and it's not undue pressure. The objective in the proposal is something God has put on our hearts, and accountability is completely reasonable.

As we'll see in Chapter 4, the relationship between the applicant and the funding agency is a partnership. They each bring specific goals, and if they overlap well enough, the agency may fund the proposal. Some church leaders have come to us and asked, "Can you help me get a grant to build a new sanctuary?" or ". . . pay the light bill?" or ". . . create a food bank?" The question is simple: How does your vision to build a new building advance an agency's goals? (It almost certainly doesn't.) Or pay the light bill? (Ditto.) But, creating a food bank may accomplish the purpose of one or several government agencies.

---

6 "AmeriCorps," AmeriCorps Fact Sheet, https://americorps.gov/sites/default/files/document/AmeriCorps-Fact-Sheet-2023.pdf.

In considering proposals to particular agencies, always ask yourself, "What will be the payoff for the agency? What is a win for them?" If you can't answer this question, don't bother submitting a proposal. They're looking for a positive impact on their target audience. If they see that your effort will accomplish that, they may release the funds you need to make it happen.

It's certainly possible that a grant can indirectly fund a project that has nothing to do with the agency. For instance, if your church has been spending $15,000 on an after-school program, you might get a grant for that purpose, which frees this money for another program in the church. So, look at what you're already doing in your community. Could you get a grant for some or all of this effort? If so, you can double your investment in the community.

Myth #8: We Tried and Failed—And I'm Not Doing That Again!

We've talked with church leaders who told us, "Yeah, I know somebody who applied for a grant but was turned down. He said he'd never make that mistake again!" When we hear this complaint, we wish we could talk to the actual person who tried and came up empty. What happened? What didn't happen? Did they actually apply, or did they quit because they didn't know what they were doing?

A couple of leaders have told us someone in their church volunteered to write a grant proposal, but it was turned down. It may be that the proposal didn't follow the agency guidelines, or the proposed program didn't align with the agency's goals.

There may be many reasons a first attempt didn't work, but that's not our experience at all. In fact, we've never been turned down. (Throughout these chapters, we often say an agency "may" fund proposals. This isn't a lack of faith. It's just the truth that not all proposals are accepted and funded . . . but all of ours have been because we've learned how to write proposals that are a win-win, and we can teach you how to do the same.)

Matthew's account of the life of Jesus tells us about many remarkable events, and one of them seems unusually strange. When Jesus and the disciples returned to Capernaum from the Mount of Transfiguration, officials from the temple asked Peter if Jesus was going to pay the temple tax. A short time later, Jesus and Peter discussed the legitimacy of the tax, but Jesus told him, "We don't want to offend them, so go down to the lake and throw in a line. Open the mouth of the first fish you catch, and you will find a large silver coin. Take it and pay the tax for both of us" (Matthew 17:27). Jesus was using an out-of-the-box funding strategy to provide for people in need—Him and Peter. It was, to say the least, unconventional. What do you think was going on in Peter's mind when he threw the line into the lake? Did he wonder if he looked like a fool? Did he have confidence that what Jesus promised He would provide? No matter what fears he may have had, he obeyed and experienced a miracle.

But there's one other point in the story: Where did the coin come from? Did a righteous person drop it in the lake? Or an unrighteous person? The source didn't matter. Jesus used an unconventional method to provide funds from an unknown source to meet a real need. Who would think to look in a fish's mouth for funding?

When we sent in our first grant proposal, it was like Peter throwing a line in the water and expecting a coin in a fish's mouth. It seemed not only new but strange. Grant funding has done wonders for Citi Church and the people of our community. It may seem unconventional, but it's a place where we can find coins.

So, here's what we want to say to you: "Come on, man! Give it a shot! Maybe this is a way God can fund programs to advance His kingdom in your community. Yes, it may be a novel thing to attempt . . . but it's not nearly as strange as going to a lake to find a coin in a fish's mouth! You can do it."

THINK ABOUT IT:

1) Do you know anyone (besides us) who has tried to get funding from a government agency or foundation? If so, what happened?

2) Which of the myths seemed most plausible before you read this chapter?

3) Did our explanation shatter the myth and give you some confidence? Why or why not?

4) Which myths still seem unsurmountable?

5) What makes them seem so formidable?

6) Did this chapter answer your questions? If not, where will you find good answers?

7) What are some specific needs in your community that God might use your church or nonprofit to meet?

SHARPEN YOUR VISION

When contestants in beauty pageants like Miss America or Miss World are asked what goal they'd like to accomplish, many of them say things like "end world hunger" or "world peace." This kind of answer may sound grand and noble on the surface, but it's far too oversimplified. It takes more to end world hunger or see world peace than making a broad, generalized statement. In our conversations with pastors and their teams, they often have broad, sweeping mission and vision statements—not as bad as the beauty contestants, but not sharp enough to galvanize their people to take bold action.

Many pastors use Jesus' answer to the Pharisee's question about the most important law and say their church's vision is to "love God and love people." Great. No problem, but how do we express that love so that it makes a difference, and who are the people at the center of the target of our efforts? When our vision statements aren't sharply focused, our efforts become scattered. As the old saying goes, "Mist in the pulpit produces fog in the pews"—and this affects our ability to reach our communities.

Mission is who you are, vision is where you're going, and strategy is how you plan to get there.

Your team needs to be crystal clear about their vision so they can coordinate everything they do to meet the objectives. If you want to apply for a grant, the agency wants to know very specifically what you're trying to accomplish with their funding. Generalities won't do.

Some people get confused about the differences and the relationships between mission, vision, and strategy. This is the way we use those terms: Mission is who you are, vision is where you're going, and strategy is how you plan to get there. Mission is your heartbeat—it doesn't change, but your vision can shift depending on changing demographics, more or fewer resources, and new opportunities. The strategy flexes depending on these and other factors. It might make it clear to begin a mission statement by saying: "We are a people who . . ."; begin a vision statement with, "We are committed to seeing God accomplish . . ."; and begin the strategic explanation with "Our specific plans to accomplish our vision include . . ."

In this chapter, we're focusing on vision. When that's in focus, leaders can strategize and use all their resources, including those they hadn't used before, to fulfill the vision God has put on their hearts. Invariably, it takes work, time, and prayer to crystallize our vision to advance God's kingdom "on earth as it is in heaven." Vision and strategy can be very effective for a season (and the season may last for many years), but significant changes require reconsideration.

In 2017, we spent months reevaluating the vision for Citi Church. It was important to revisit our commitments even if we hadn't altered course, but we realized we had opportunities and challenges at that point in our history we hadn't experienced in the early years. We were no longer in the pioneering phase; we had become established, with a clear and strong culture, so it was time to shift into a higher gear. Continually writing grant proposals helped us clarify our vision because we had to state, over and over again, what we specifically planned to accomplish with the funds. It was the chicken and the egg: We had to have a clear vision to submit the proposals but writing them inspired us to keep dreaming bigger dreams.

We consulted with a pastor and his team to talk about using grants to fund a school they wanted to start. Their vision was like ours: to use the school as an opportunity to serve kids and their parents, build relationships, and invite them to trust Jesus and come to the church. But there was a problem: The church's bylaws specifically limited the school to kids of members in the church. By the church's guidelines, they were prevented from reaching out to people in the neighborhood. They needed to go back to the basics and reestablish the mission, vision, and guiding principles of the church.

Crafting a compelling vision requires two things: *prayer* that seeks the heart of God for clear direction and *hard work* to evaluate the needs and opportunities in the community. Out of the push and pull of those factors, a clear vision will surface. It's not enough to copy the vision statement of Andy Stanley, Robert Morris, or Steven Furtick. This requires real work and real prayer.

A mission organization in the Northwest called to ask us to help with grant proposals. We were happy to talk with them. When we asked them to tell us their vision, the director waited a few seconds to collect his thoughts, and then he said, "We want to reach people with the gospel."

"Great. What people?"

"Well, all people."

"Yes, of course, but where are you focusing your efforts?"

"I'm not sure what you mean."

"Where are you sending your staff members?"

"All over the world."

By this point, we were starting to understand the problem. "So, how's it going?"

"Not so well," he said sadly. "We're spread so thin that we're not making much of a difference anywhere."

Bingo.

The leader of another organization asked for advice about securing grant money to feed homeless people in their community. "Great. That's a clear vision. How will you accomplish it? Agencies will want to know how you plan to fulfill this goal."

"We'll give them food."

"Yes, I'm sure you will. Who will you serve? Where are they? What's their condition? How often will you provide meals? Where will you get nourishing food for them? What's your delivery system? How will you measure success?"

The director looked at us with wide eyes and said, "I don't know. I don't know the answers to *any* of those questions. That's why I asked for your help."

When we went on our prayer walks in the first months we were in Miami, we heard the same concern over and over again: the kids feel hopeless, they don't have adequate resources, and it's easy for them to drop out of school and make a mess of their lives. God made it very clear that for Citi Church, the center of the target is the "next generation" and, secondly, their families. Virtually every decision we make, every plan we outline, and every effort of our team is directed to this primary and secondary audience. After-school programs, tutoring, summer camps, and hiring gifted staff to work with children and teenagers are at the heart of Citi Church.

Habakkuk was God's prophet during a turbulent time in the history of His people. He lived when the kingdom was divided and Babylon's power was rising east of the Promised Land. Judah had gone off the rails, worshipping Baal, sacrificing children to Molech, and abandoning the temple. This was happening as Assyria ruled over the land for a hundred years. In the first chapter, Habakkuk complained that nothing was going right, and he pleaded with God to show up and turn things around. God's answer wasn't what the prophet expected. Yes, things were bad, but they were soon going to be far worse! If you think the Assyrians are terrible, you don't know what the Babylonians will do! In response, Habakkuk again pleaded with God, reminding Him of His power and holiness, as well as the plight of the people, helpless unless God intervenes. His question was, "Why does such evil go unpunished?"

> **Ultimately, God will act—often not in the way we expected, and rarely in the timetable we hoped . . . but He will answer.**

Again, God didn't answer the way Habakkuk expected, but the prophet was resolute in his faith. He declared,

"I will stand at my watch and station myself on the ramparts; I will look to see what he will say to me, and what answer I am to give to this complaint" (Habakkuk 2:1, NIV).

And God answered:

> *Write down the revelation and make it plain on tablets so that a herald may run with it. For the revelation awaits an appointed time; it speaks of the end and will not prove false. Though it linger, wait for it; it will certainly come and will not delay. —vv. 2-3 (NIV)*

The very act of writing forces us to be more precise. The act of communicating it to others forces us to fine-tune it and own it. The act of waiting tests our dependence and patience as we keep looking to God when He seems to not be paying attention. Ultimately, God will act—often not in the way we expected, and rarely in the timetable we hoped ... but He will answer. That's His promise.

Agencies expect us to communicate a clear purpose so they can determine if we're a good partner for them. The alignment doesn't have to be absolutely perfect, like stacking Legos, but it needs to be complementary. For instance, a church has a vision to reach and disciple young men. Their thinking is that if they can reach that audience, the men will bring their wives, children, and girlfriends, and someday, they'll become pillars in the church. The pastor established a strong ministry of mentoring these men, and he submitted a proposal to an agency that funds courses on financial management. Learning to manage money is certainly an aspect of becoming a godly disciple. It wasn't at the center of the church's efforts, but it was a corollary, and the young men became better husbands, fathers, and disciples.

ELEVATOR PITCH

We need to be able to articulate a clear vision in thirty seconds, the time it takes to go up or down a floor or two on an elevator. If we can do that, we can share it with anyone at almost any time. Also, we'll feel more confident in our ability to communicate with people, and they'll catch a glimpse of our hearts and our plans.

I (Tony) am working with an organization in Nicaragua to train pastors. My elevator pitch is: "We're a network that connects pastors to other pastors so they can effectively collaborate to expand their churches and the kingdom. We do this through programs, entrepreneur incubators, pastors' gatherings, and collective outreaches." (I might have a few seconds left over!)

Our church's vision statement is very short but very clear: "At Citi Church, generations are equipped to be Christ-minded, life-giving people who live with purpose." If I want to explain a little more, I say, "We sponsor the South Florida School of Ministry and Citi Christian Academy, and we serve young people and their families."

It's important to have a vision statement on the tips of our tongues. Nehemiah models this process: During the reign of the Babylonian king Artaxerxes, Hanani arrived in Babylon and told Nehemiah about the plight of God's people in Judah. "Things are not going well for those who returned to the province of Judah. They are in great trouble and disgrace. The wall of Jerusalem has been torn down, and the gates have been destroyed by fire" (Nehemiah 1:3). The news broke his heart, and he fasted and prayed for days. He confessed the sins of his people and praised God for his unfailing love. He asked God to hear his prayer that the king would be favorable to him.

Nehemiah was the king's cupbearer, an honored and responsible position because kings were afraid someone would try to poison them. The king noticed that Nehemiah looked heartbroken, so he asked in 2:2, "Why are you looking so sad? You don't look sick to me. You must be deeply troubled." (Pretty perceptive, King!)

Nehemiah knew that speaking the truth might cost him his life, but he didn't hesitate: "Long live the king! How can I not be sad? For the city where my ancestors are buried is in ruins, and the gates have been destroyed by fire" (v. 3).

He must have been stunned by the king's reply: "Well, how can I help you?" (v. 4)

Nehemiah shared his elevator pitch: "If it please the king, and if you are pleased with me, your servant, send me to Judah to rebuild the city where my ancestors are buried" (v. 5). The king asked a couple of questions and then gave him permission to rebuild the shattered walls, including safe passage to Jerusalem, and all the resources he would need to complete the task. That's an effective pitch!

Leaders who are content with a general vision statement don't get up in the morning excited about seeing the next answer to prayer and the provisions God has provided. Everything seems equally important, and it's easy to get bogged down in managing problems instead of staying focused on possibilities. Lack of clarity makes the leader frustrated, and the team gets frustrated, too.

We're part of the body of Christ. That means we all play a vital role, but our roles aren't the same. Each of us has to discern what God has called us to be and do, and then we can do it with all our hearts. I (Tony) am not the answer for the whole world, but God can make me an effective part of his body to make a difference where he directs me.

Leaders who have a clear vision learn one of the most important words in leadership: "No." Business executives talk about "opportunity costs." When we say "yes" to an opportunity, we necessarily say "no" to many more possibilities. This is true for investors, business leaders who make decisions about products, and pastors who choose the one central thing God has called them to do over the dozens of good things they could do (and others want them to do).

A clear vision inspires people, focuses resources, and produces measurable results. When people in the pews know their time as volunteers and their contributions to the church are paying big dividends, they want to serve and give even more. And when grant funders see us as effective and trustworthy, they consider us to be valued partners and usually extend the grants to the next cycle.

I understand the pressure to do too much. Early in my career, I thought I could do everything. I ran around playing whack-a-mole to deal with all the problems. I felt frustrated and exhausted, and Dianna wondered if I'd ever slow down.

A seminary professor commented that the goal of every church is to "establish outposts for the kingdom." I like that concept, but outposts look different in different places. Kingdom presence for the homeless and hungry has particular characteristics, and kingdom presence in a pastor's training ministry looks quite different, but in every setting, we represent our King. In his second letter to the Corinthians, Paul explained that each of us is an ambassador to the "foreign land" near our homes:

And all of this is a gift from God, who brought us back
to Himself through Christ. And God has given us this
task of reconciling people to Him. For God was in
Christ, reconciling the world to Himself, no longer
counting people's sins against them. And he gave
us this wonderful message of reconciliation. So we
are Christ's ambassadors; God is making his appeal
through us. We speak for Christ when we plead,
"Come back to God!" For God made Christ, who
never sinned, to be the offering for our sin, so that
we could be made right with God through Christ.
—2 Corinthians 5:18-21

A US ambassador to the United Arab Emirates has a vision for his role that fits the needs of that wealthy Arab nation, but the vision of the ambassador to Bolivia is aware of a very different set of needs. Each one represents the United States to the leaders and the people where they serve, but they have particular goals to meet specific needs in those nations.

God has led us to find resources in unexpected places.

At Citi Church, our vision is to be God's ambassadors to the next generation, and the audience in our community is mostly recent immigrants. So, our target audience is young people and their families who have very few resources. How do you build a movement of God there? One person who heard us speak laughed and said, "That sure seems like a losing formula for a church plant!" It would be, but God has led us to find resources in unexpected places. At a conference, the head of the church planting network for a major denomination heard what we're doing and asked, "How in the world are you making this work?" Our answer: only by the grace of God, a little creative imagination, and the diligence to jump through a few hoops to get the funding we need. We're ambassadors to an underserved and marginalized culture, so we have to trust God to give us wisdom and favor and open doors with grant funders who will see us as trusted partners.

KEY QUESTIONS

When we speak at events for leaders or consult with pastors and their teams, we usually ask some questions to help them clarify and narrow their focus, such as:

> ➤ What is your mission?
>
> If someone cuts you, what do you bleed? Who are you? What makes you tick? What are the words that describe your church in every conceivable activity, from staff meetings to worship to outreaches in the community?
>
> These questions define your reason for existence, your heartbeat, and your culture.

> ➤ What is the vision God has put on your heart?
>
> Is it actually a God-given vision, or is it something you've adopted from someone else? How much have you wrestled with this question? In ten or twenty years, what do you want the reputation of your church to be?

➤ Why does the vision matter?

What will be the impact on your community and the body of Christ? If you didn't exist, what hole would you leave?

➤ Who is at the center of your target?

If you say it's "everybody," take some time to think more carefully. What demographic group is in the center, who is one ring out, and who is two rings out? Who in the community are the multipliers? If they come to faith in Christ, they'll bring others. Who are the stakeholders, the keepers of the vision?

➤ What will success look like?

In one year? In five years? In ten years? In twenty years? If you can't imagine the fulfillment of your vision and articulate it so that it captures hearts, you'll be content just running nice programs and keeping people comfortable.

The pastor, board members, and staff team of a church in Missouri went through this process early in their history, and God led them to focus on thirty-five-year-old men as the center of the target. Their sermon illustrations, programs, and intentional discipleship strategy were all tailored to young men who could bring their families into the life of the church. If you stand in their lobby on any Sunday morning, you'll see hundreds of young men, their wives, and a zillion children. The church is now thirty years old, and many of those who were young at the outset of the church are seasoned, visionary leaders, and they're still focused on young men and their families. Over the years, the target audience hasn't changed.

EXAMPLES OF CLARIFIED VISIONS

We've worked with many churches and nonprofit organizations to help them sharpen the vision of what God has called them to do. In these examples, we've changed the names, but the vision statements are good, clear, and compelling:

➤ Community Bridge Fellowship: "To foster a vibrant community space where individuals of all ages can connect, share in faith, and grow together, building a harmonious and inclusive future."

➤ Hope for Tomorrow Foundation: "To empower underprivileged youth with education, mentorship, and community involvement, shaping a future where every child has the tools they need to succeed."

➤ Green Earth Initiative: "To educate communities on sustainable living practices, working toward a future where humans live in harmony with nature for a healthier planet."

➤ Brighter Futures Children's Home: "To provide a safe, nurturing, and loving environment for children in need, paving the way for a future where all children can thrive and chase their dreams."

➤ Wells of Hope Outreach: "To bring clean water and vital health education to remote communities, envisioning a future where every family has the resources they need to maintain their health."

➤ Mosaic Arts Collective: "To bring communities together through the power of art and creativity, fostering unity and understanding among diverse groups."

➤ New Beginnings Job Network: "To empower individuals facing life challenges, like addiction or incarceration, by providing them with the skills and support they need to find employment and contribute positively to society."

➤ How do you know when your hard work to clarify your church's vision has paid off? When it's so clear and compelling that it inspires your creativity and prompts you to pray, trusting God to do something so wonderful that you could never do it on your own.

NO COASTING ALLOWED

We understand. Tending God's sheep is often tiring and discouraging work. Many pastors and other leaders are giving it their all . . . and more than their all. A recent Barna survey found that more than four in ten pastors are so burned out and discouraged that they're considering leaving the ministry. The report states: "Over half of pastors who have considered quitting full-time ministry (56 percent) say the 'immense stress of the job' has factored into their thoughts on leaving. Beyond these general stressors, two in five pastors (43 percent) say 'I feel lonely and isolated' while 38 percent name 'current political divisions' as reasons they've considered stepping away."[7] It's very difficult to be an inspiring leader when you have one foot out the door!

---

7 "Pastors Share Top Reasons They've Considered Quitting the Ministry in the Past Year," Barna, 27 April 2022, https://www.barna.com/research/pastors-quitting-ministry/.

It's better to craft something that captures your heart, gives you hope that your church can make a huge difference, and inspires your people to give their best to advance God's purposes.

There is no question that we live and serve in trying times. Pastors are sitting targets every Sunday morning, and as our culture becomes more caustic, many who claim to love God are becoming more critical. Under all the pressure—including difficulties at home—leaders can become more cautious, defensive, and unwilling to try anything that might create even more pushback and stress. It's easier to coast, not making waves.

We believe the current state of our culture makes it even more crucial for pastors and their teams to do the work to clarify their vision, to pray, fast, and dream God's dreams for their flocks and their communities. Then, armed with the direction and the power of God, they can reach out to the lost and the least, build multiplying disciples, have a profound impact on their communities, and send committed believers to mission fields near and far.

A vision statement that sounds like poetry may not be the answer (unless you're leading an art institute). It's better to craft something that captures your heart, gives you hope that your church can make a huge difference, and inspires your people to give their best to advance God's purposes.

THINK ABOUT IT:

1) How do you distinguish between mission, vision, and strategy?

2) Has the distinction been helpful to you? Why or why not?

3) If not, do our definitions and distinctions help?

4) How often do you think about (and pray according to) your church's vision statement?

5) How does (or might) seeing each person in the church as an ambassador help to clarify your vision?

6) What was Nehemiah's "elevator pitch"?

7) Take some time to think, pray, and discuss the key questions about vision.

CHAPTER 4

WIN-WIN-WIN

The inherent question every grant funder asks when organizations submit grant proposals is: "Why would we write you a check?" The question forces us to see the partnership from their point of view. We have to clearly articulate how our program or service accomplishes their objective. A pervasive and often unspoken sentiment among many in the charitable and faith-based sectors is the belief that grant funders operate from a position of skepticism and reservation.

Many see grant funders as adversaries: distant overseers, fierce guardians of their resources, looking down with skepticism upon our aspirations. If we see them that way, we certainly won't value them as partners. When we submit a grant proposal, we're not looking for a fight, and we're not trying to twist anyone's arm. Instead, we're looking for organizations that care about the same things we do and value them as partners.

Some church leaders want complete autonomy . . . to accomplish their purpose on their own, so when they go to an agency to ask for funding, they can come across as both arrogant and narrow—arrogant because they don't communicate their need for partners and narrow because they're focused only on their own goals and programs, giving little thought to the agency's stated goals.

Good partnerships with funding agencies create a win-win-win. The church has an effective outreach into the community to build relationships and credibility, the agency accomplishes its goals, and the people's needs are met. When this happens, the recipients of love want to know more about the people who have gone out of their way to care for them in tangible ways.

We can accomplish far more with partners than we can on our own. One day, Jesus taught a crowd on the shore of the Sea of Galilee. He saw two boats at the water's edge, and He asked one of the fishermen, Simon Peter, if He could borrow his boat. Jesus pushed the boat out a little way from the shore and sat down to teach. The sound carried well over the water, and everyone could hear Him. When He finished speaking, Jesus turned to Peter and told him, "Put out into deep water, and let down the nets for a catch."

Peter was initially reluctant: "Master we've worked hard all night and haven't caught anything." But something in this preacher melted his resistance: "But because you say so, I will let down the nets."

Peter and Andrew let down their nets—at a time in the day when fish typically can't be caught because they go to deeper, cooler water. Suddenly, they had so many fish in their nets that they began to break! They called the men from the other boat, James and John, to help them. They rowed out to them, and the four of them hauled in so many fish that their boats began to sink! (If you're a fisherman, you dream about days like that!)

Peter realized this wasn't just luck—it was a miracle. Instantly, he realized he wasn't worthy of this kind of blessing, so he insisted, "Go away from me, Lord; I am a sinful man!"

Jesus told Peter, "Don't be afraid; from now on you will fish for people."

Luke tells us, "So they pulled their boats up on shore, left everything and followed him" (Luke 5:1-11, NIV).

Peter kept far more fish that day because he had skilled, eager partners—his brother, James, and John. And, of course, the source of the resources, Jesus, played the starring role in the miracle. The results: the four men were astonished and followed Jesus, Jesus now had a third of His discipleship group, and the fish undoubtedly fed a lot of hungry people.

Citi Church joins other organizations to meet the needs of the city. For these particular efforts, our shirts and fliers don't just have our church's logo on them; they sometimes have ten or twelve logos and names. Together, we make a bigger impact, so we're willing to be one part of the outreach instead of insisting on doing it alone.

BIG DOORS, SMALL HINGES

Quite often, seemingly insignificant aspects of a strategy make a huge difference. For instance, one of the most pervasive problems in underserved and marginalized communities is the curse of generational poverty. In middle- and upper-class parts of the city, when a young person needs a job, she asks a respected person in the community—often friends of her parents—to introduce her to the CEO, sometimes bypassing the HR process. But this doesn't happen in areas like ours. Marginalized people don't often have those connections, so they usually walk in without a personal recommendation. This limits opportunities and discourages those who desperately need good jobs so they can provide for their families and, often, their extended families.

When we hire a staff member, we provide a course on the impact of generational poverty so our new hire will understand this nagging problem in our culture. It's called "A Framework for Understanding Poverty"[8] by Dr. Ruby K. Payne. She teaches that there are two types of poverty: generational and situational. Generational poverty exists when two or more generations of a family live in constant want; situational poverty is the result of an event, such as divorce, sickness, or business bankruptcy. This understanding inspires compassion, but it also stimulates creative ideas about helping people break out of the cycle of hopelessness. Good intentions aren't enough. We've found ways to educate, train, and equip people so they can take big steps to be financially stable.

One of the most common assumptions is that people living in poverty long to move into the middle class, but that's not always true. When middle-class people with a lack of understanding try to help those in poverty, they can come across as condescending and send the message that those

---

8 Dr. Ruby K. Payne, "A Framework for Understanding Poverty: 10 Actions to Educate Students," on-demand workshop, 3 hr., 24 min.

in poverty are "less than" and need to be rescued, while seeing themselves as wiser, older siblings, or even saviors. With this mindset, those who are trying to help can do more harm than good.

People who feel stuck in generational poverty need two things: education and relationships. They need information about themselves, the job market, interviewing tips, and the jobs they want to find, and they need supportive relationships with people who know them, understand their hopes and fears, and can open a door or two for them. To find out more, go to www.ahaprocess.com.

FINDING GREAT PARTNERS

The old saying is that to *find* the right person to marry, you need to *be* the right person. The same is true in nonprofit-grant partnerships. It's important to look in the mirror to see who you are and how well your church works outside its walls. You may need to take some time to address any arrogance, superiority, paternalism, or insistence on autonomy. (Don't assume they don't exist in you or your church culture.) Church leaders who work well with agencies have a powerful blend of humility, courage, vision, attention to detail, and persistence.

Then, to find agencies who can become (and remain for years) valued partners, consider these points:

> Agencies that provide grants aren't distant entities holding the purse strings. They are potential allies, waiting to join hands with us in our mission. They, too, want to produce a positive impact, and their primary goal is to find partners like us who can make that change possible.

Agencies that provide grants aren't distant entities holding the purse strings. They are potential allies, waiting to join hands with us in our mission.

➢ When we view them as partners, we unlock a collaborative relationship rich in shared expertise, resources, and mutual respect. The leaders of those agencies often become trusted friends. C. S. Lewis's description of friendship fits here:

> *Friendship arises out of mere Companionship when two or more of the companions discover that they have in common some insight or interest or even taste which the others do not share and which, till that moment, each believed to be his own unique treasure (or burden). The typical expression of opening Friendship would be something like, "What? You too? I thought I was the only one."*[9]

➢ That's how we feel when we develop relationships with the officials at agencies, especially when they renew their grants year after year.

➢ The agency's success is intricately tied to ours. When our projects thrive, it validates their faith in us, and it

---

9   C. S. Lewis, The Four Loves (New York, NY: Harper Collins, 1960).

solidifies their role in catalyzing positive change. Rather than seeing them as mere gatekeepers, we recognize them as co-laborers.

➤ Through collaboration, we can ensure that our vision isn't just a dream but a shared goal that we're collectively striving to realize . . . and we celebrate together.

Friends take care of friends. Early in Citi Church's history, we received funding through the federal No Child Left Behind Act (this story is in Chapter 1), which was administered through the state of Florida. Our proposal, the funding, and our work in the schools established a good relationship with officials in the Miami-Dade County School District and, specifically, in the Title One Department that provided programs for low-income students who were deemed at risk for low academic achievement. However, after the next election, the federal program and funding ended. Fast forward several years . . . The county school superintendent allocated money for the Million Dollar Literacy Project, but by that time, we were out of this particular loop, so we didn't hear about the meeting for organizations that were interested in the project. One of our contacts in the department realized we hadn't attended and called us to encourage us to come to the meeting, which was still in progress. She asked me (Keisha), "Where are you?"

I answered, "What are you talking about? Where am I supposed to be?"

She told me about the program and the meeting, and then she insisted, "You better get over here . . . fast!"

We dropped everything we were doing, jumped in the car, and drove ten minutes to the building. Thankfully, the meeting hadn't ended yet. We applied for the grant and received over $250,000 of the allocated million dollars. This literacy project was different from No Child Left Behind. For that one, our focus was on tutoring kids in reading and math, but officials realized they also needed to help the parents so they could oversee and reinforce their children's progress. To accomplish that goal, we hosted "Literacy Nights" for whole families, encouraged them to read, and gave parents books in English and Spanish so they could read to their kids.

This blessing happened because we found friends everywhere we went. Our desire is summed up in the explicit questions we ask people who run agencies: "What can we do to make your job easier? How can we partner with you to fulfill your goals?"

In 2013, we launched Citi Christian Academy, a private Christian school at Citi Church. Three years later, we got a call from the school district to tell us we were eligible for Title One funding. They explained that private schools teaching low-income kids could receive funds just like public schools. We used the funds for computers and other technology, psychological assessments, and a tutoring program. We had no idea this money was available, and we wouldn't have gotten it if someone we'd served years before hadn't called to let us know.

An official from a local school district called us recently to ask if we'd partner with the school board to sponsor classes for English as a Second Language for adults. The official said, "You have a status in the community we don't have. We know that if we want this program to be a success, we need you as our partner."

I (Keisha) got a call from the school district to ask if we'd coach two people who had just received contracts to work with the school district. One of the ladies had called the district several times to ask questions, but finally, the district official decided she needed more than answers to a few questions. She needed a mentor, and they asked us to provide that service. They see us as an asset, as people who have shared values and are committed to excellence, and they asked us to show these two how we relate to them. What a surprise! What an honor! The message I wanted to impart to her was this: "Plan well. Organize your people and your resources. Do what you say you'll do. Send in reports on time. Don't take shortcuts. Serve with excellence. Do it right because you're not just representing your organization; you're representing the King and His kingdom. As you work with them, you're giving secular people a picture of Jesus. Don't forget that."

One year, Wilfredo "Willy" Gort, the city commissioner who represented our part of Miami, began an outreach to distribute backpacks to kids when they started school. That first year, it was chaotic. Security was deficient, so kids were grabbing as much as they could carry and running away. Police officers tried to control the crowd, but a crackdown just made things worse. I (Tony) talked to the commissioner and made this offer: "Next year, we'll handle security. You can bring one police officer, but he can stay in the background. Leave everything to us." Twelve months later, our team was in the street and parking lot directing traffic, and others from our church distributed the backpacks. Everything went very smoothly. The commissioner was so happy (and relieved) with our efforts that we became his partner at the beginning of every school year and future Christmas outreaches. Of course, we wore our Citi Church t-shirts so people knew we were serving them and their children. He told me, "When people see your shirts, they say, 'That's Citi Church! That's my church!'" The irony is that many of them had never walked through the doors of our church, but they felt connected to us because they saw us serving them in different ways throughout the community. Whenever that commissioner had any big event, he asked us to help provide traffic control and security.

When organizations reach out beyond their walls and care for the people God loves, He delights to partner with them to provide in amazing ways.

A couple of years later, we expanded our school to a larger building. I (Dianna) discovered a problem with zoning related to a certificate of use. I immediately called the commissioner to ask for his help, and he jumped in to solve the problem. He rallied his team to contact city departments to let them know who we were and asked for their assistance in resolving our situation. Some of them even called me to say, "The commissioner called me to ask for my help. When can I come to see you so we can solve this problem?" In a short time, all the permits were granted, and we were on our way.

Building relationships of trust and respect with officials and grant funders has opened doors we didn't even know existed. We've had more resources to serve kids and their parents, and our community is the beneficiary.

When organizations reach out beyond their walls and care for the people God loves, He delights to partner with them to provide in amazing ways. God's justice isn't just punishing the guilty; it's also caring for those who are vulnerable: the poor, widows, the unemployed, immigrants, orphans, addicts, homeless people, and everyone else who is at the end of their rope. In everything we do, we want God to be the center, the heart, and the power. One of the historians of the Old Testament reminds us, "For the eyes of the LORD run to and fro throughout the whole earth, to show Himself strong on behalf of those whose heart is loyal to Him" (2 Chronicles 16:9, NKJV).

As we've tried to follow the Lord to reach deep into the fabric of our community, God has poured out His blessings on us. We've developed wonderful partnerships with grant funders, many of the officials have become trusted friends, and the programs God has put on our hearts have touched tens of thousands of lives.

THINK ABOUT IT:

1) How do you respond when people take you for granted or feel entitled to you fixing their problems? How do you think government officials or grant funders respond when they're treated this way?

2) What are some ways you can "look in the mirror" to see if you and your church will be a good partner?

3) What do you think you'll find?

4) What difference does it make to see grant funders as allies instead of adversaries?

5) Look back at the section on "Finding Great Partners." Which of these stands out to you?

6) Does the idea of doing the work for a win-win-win excite you, inspire you, scare you, exhaust you, or bore you? Explain your answer.

CHAPTER 5

TREASURES IN
THE DIRT

A church leader heard our story and asked, "When you started to send grant proposals and the funding started to flow, did you stop and realize someone had strengths in this area you hadn't noticed before?"

My (Dianna's) answer was, "Yes, that 'someone' was all three of us! The idea of getting money from grant funders had never crossed our minds. The entire world of grant funding was foreign to us. We'd been involved in churches and church planting, so we assumed all the money had to come from tithes and offerings, and most of the manpower would come from volunteers. When Yvonne introduced us to the concept of grant funding, initially, we had a lot of reservations and questions [including all the myths we described in Chapter 2]. We needed answers to a lot of questions before we could move forward with this crazy idea. Were there people who were surprised to find out they had strengths in this area? Yes, all of us."

Let me back up and tell a little more about the background of the story we shared earlier in the book. One of Tony's brothers, Manny, is a pastor, and he introduced us to an accountant, Ero Torrales, who had been working with Hope for Miami (formerly known as Family & Children Faith Coalition), an organization that "nurtures children and youth through effective programs to help them build positive, healthy futures."[10] Ero connected us to Yvonne Sawyer. Yvonne explained how grants funded the organization, and she introduced us to the idea that we could apply for grants that would pay for after-school programs in local churches like ours. The grants would pay for the employees, all the supplies, and utilities. The church only needed to provide the facilities. This idea fit perfectly with our vision to reach children and, through them, their families. That was always our vision to reach our part of Miami, and suddenly, we had an effective, funded strategy that would build our credibility among naturally suspicious people.

At first, Yvonne secured the grant, and we worked under her auspices. We worked hard that summer to reach children in our community and meet the goals and deadlines for Family & Children Faith Coalition (now, Hope for Miami) summer camp. After a year and a half, she encouraged us to apply for a grant on our own. She coached us through the initial process and gave us feedback as we wrote our proposal, and we never looked back. Yvonne opened our eyes to a brand-new world.

---

10 "Who We Are," Hope for Miami, https://www.hopeformiami.org/.

We will forever be grateful for the way God used Yvonne Sawyer to show us the path that she pioneered. Thank you, Yvonne!

In a series of Jesus' parables, Matthew records a short one about an accidental discovery: "The kingdom of heaven is like treasure hidden in a field. When a man found it, he hid it again, and then in his joy went and sold all he had and bought that field" (Matthew 13:44, NIV). In those days, Palestine was a battleground for armies coming from the north, east, and south, including the Persians, Greeks, Egyptians, and Romans. People who saw an army coming needed to hide their most valuable possessions, and one of the ways was to put them in a box and hide them in a field where the ground had already been disturbed by plowing so a fresh hole wouldn't be noticed. Jesus' story is about a man who was simply walking from one place to another, and on the way, he noticed something unusual in the dirt. Maybe a recent rain had exposed the box. It could have been there for decades and maybe even longer. It was obvious that the current owner of the land wasn't aware of it, so the man gladly sold all he had and bought the land. He found treasure in the dirt, just like we discovered strengths we didn't know we had and we uncovered sources of funding we didn't know existed.

OUR "WHY"

When you plant a church in a part of a city where people live in poverty, and they don't trust anyone from the outside, you need God to give you some creative ways to fund the ministry. When Yvonne introduced us to the concept of grant funding, we overcame our initial reluctance because we had no other options. Other communities may have wealth, so people can give out of their abundance, but people in our neighborhood were barely scraping by. As the saying goes, "Desperate times call for desperate measures." To put our predicament in a biblical context, we relied on Paul's perspective. When all hope seemed to be lost, God spoke to him:

> But he said to me, "My grace is sufficient for you, for my power is made perfect in weakness." Therefore I will boast all the more gladly about my weaknesses, so that Christ's power may rest on me. That is why, for Christ's sake, I delight in weaknesses, in insults, in hardships, in persecutions, in difficulties. For when I am weak, then I am strong. —2 Corinthians 12:9-10 (NIV)

Our weakness prompted us to be open to a new idea to fund our ministry and create effective ways to serve the people around us. Would we have jumped at the chance if we had plenty of money? Maybe, maybe not, but that wasn't a luxury we could lean on.

We weren't afraid to "try something" to see if it would work. In fact, every new grant proposal is based on experimentation, creativity, and hope.

When Franklin D. Roosevelt became president in 1933, the nation was in the middle of the Great Depression. In the days before his inauguration, banks all over the country failed because people had no more confidence in them and withdrew their money. When the banks ran out of money, some people left empty-handed, losing everything. Roosevelt encouraged the crowd that day: "We have nothing to fear but fear itself."[11] But his solution to the nation's enormous financial problems wasn't just words; it was action. His "New Deal" created many new agencies in government to strengthen the economy, put people back to work, and put money in their pockets so they could buy necessities. Some of the programs were spectacular successes; some were failures. He explained his perspective at a commencement address at Oglethorpe University in Atlanta: "This country needs and, unless I mistake its temper, the country demands bold, persistent experimentation. It is common sense to take a method and try it. If it fails, admit it frankly and try another. But above all, try something."[12]

We weren't afraid to "try something" to see if it would work. In fact, every new grant proposal is based on experimentation, creativity, and hope. If any of them hadn't worked, we wouldn't have quit; we would have just "admitted it frankly and tried another."

---

11 Franklin D. Roosevelt, "We have nothing to fear but fear itself," VisualParadigm Online, https://online.visual-paradigm.com/flipbook-maker/templates/quotes/we-have-nothing-to-fear-but-fear-itself-franklin-d-roosevelt/.
12 Debbie Aiken, "Remembering FDR's Commencement Address at Oglethorpe," Oglethorpe, 22 May 2012, https://source.oglethorpe.edu/2012/05/22/remembering-fdrs-commencement-speech-at-oglethorpe/

We had a small team at that point: Natasha White, Stephanie McNeil, Debra Oliva, Chad and "Baby" Pelham, and Andrea Jolly—and all of us were eager to learn. We were (and are) full of optimism—not that everything will go perfectly, but that God will open doors. If one is closed, He'll open another one. When the Lord opened the door for after-school programs, it was a perfect fit. All of us had been involved in education as teachers in elementary schools, junior high, and the college level, so we had experience we could rely on. I (Keisha) have a degree in engineering from Clemson University. When I joined the team, I thought my engineering expertise was going to be put on a shelf and forgotten, but I soon realized I could use the same analytical processes in my work at the church. In engineering, you have a goal, and you work with the constraints of the materials to devise a solution. I just had to re-contextualize what I'd learned in the School of Engineering. At the church, we had goals, and we had constraints, so we had to find creative solutions . . . and a big solution was grant funding. For me, it was like solving an engineering problem. Dianna sees holes Pastor Tony and I don't see, so she plays a crucial role in making sure all the details are taken care of.

Taking risks to start new ventures is part of my (Tony's) DNA. My father was an entrepreneur. He began as a migrant field hand when he was fourteen years old, and he traveled around the country to pick crops as each one ripened. He knew that wasn't his future, so he left the fields and got a factory job in New York with Levolor Brothers, the company that makes blinds for windows. His supervisors were two Italian men who saw potential in him, so they helped him get his GED and enroll in a vocational school teaching auto body repair. When he graduated, he got a job at a body shop, and after a year, he realized he could manage his own company. He started his shop in New Jersey.

After a few years, he moved to Puerto Rico and built a very large body shop with his brothers. He then left the shop with his brothers and moved to Clewiston, Florida, a town of about 8,000 then . . . and the same size today. On his first visit there, he told himself, *This is a beautiful little town. Someday I'm going to raise my family here.* We moved there, he opened a body shop and was successful because he got contracts with the county to work on all their vehicles. He also opened a used car lot. His goal was that all his seven children would go to college and graduate.

When he was fifty-five, he sold his shop. He moved to Venezuela and opened an orphanage, but when Chavez took over, the government took control of the orphanage and kicked him out. He moved to Honduras and started another orphanage. Later, he left a church in charge of it, and today, my father is a missionary in the Andean Mountains of Peru. At seventy-eight years old, he planted a church at an elevation of 14,000 feet and started another orphanage and a home for the elderly. Most of the people live below the elevation of the church, but on Sundays, they walk up the mountain to worship Jesus with my dad.

My father reminds me of Caleb, one of only two spies who gave a good report to Moses when he sent them to survey the Promised Land. The other ten said the enemies were too strong, but Caleb never lost his optimism and courage. Forty-five years later, when he was eighty-five, Caleb told the people,

> Now then, just as the Lord promised, he has kept me alive for forty-five years since the time he said this to Moses, while Israel moved about in the wilderness. So here I am today, eighty-five years old! I am still as strong today as the day Moses sent me out; I'm just as vigorous to go out to battle now as I was then. Now give me this hill country that the Lord promised me that day. You yourself heard then that the Anakites were there and their cities were large and fortified, but, the Lord helping me, I will drive them out just as he said. —Joshua 14:10-12 (NIV)

"Give me this hill country"—not the land that's most conducive to agriculture, but land that requires extra work to make it profitable. Caleb wasn't looking for an easy life. He just wanted to make an impact, no matter what it took. That's the spirit of my father, and I was inspired as I watched him always reaching for more, stretching himself to advance the kingdom of God.

PRACTICAL STEPS

We encourage leaders to engage their teams in some activities that can sweep some dirt away so they can uncover hidden treasures of gifts, strengths, and passions. We recommend:

> ➤ Focus groups of four to twenty people can meet to study the needs of the community, reveal their talents, and look for opportunities to make a difference. They can also

discuss how existing efforts are successful and how to expand them, as well as why efforts aren't as productive as they hoped.

➤ A SWOT analysis is common in the business world, but many organizations and churches seldom examine the team's strengths, weaknesses, opportunities, and threats. Quite often, this conversation surfaces underutilized strengths and passions of at least a few people on the team and identifies open doors of opportunity in the community.

➤ Many teams benefit from conducting a skills inventory for each member, which examines talents, education, and experiences. When the vision is compelling, and people are taking risks, skills surface naturally, but at the beginning, it may be helpful to use a tool to identify latent talents. Several inventories are available online, or you can use one of them as a template to create your own.

➤ Spiritual gifts assessments help people identify their God-given talents, and when these are confirmed by others in the group who have seen these in action, people feel deeply affirmed and empowered.

➤ Personality assessments are especially helpful in forming stronger relationships. When people understand each other's motivations and desires, they don't make as many negative assumptions.

We find it very helpful for teams to use a combination of these inventories so they get different perspectives on themselves and each other. Many conflicts on teams are the result of misplaced assumptions (that others are just like us) and misunderstandings. These assessments open the door for conversations so the team can function more effectively. We recommend these tools to every team within an organizational structure. The team in every department can be more effective if they understand what makes each other tick.

For a list of resources we have used and recommend, scan this QR Code now.

As we've consulted with organizations and churches and talked about uncovering hidden treasures in their teams, some of the leaders have been surprised when a team member pointed out the underused strength of another person on the team. Going through the process of looking for treasures in the dirt has many benefits, especially the affirmation people feel when others confirm their strengths, realizing someone needs a different role to match their talents, understanding each other to minimize tension, and the fun of self-discovery.

RELATED TO GRANTS

Agencies that can fund our programs want to know if we're capable, so we include the particular strengths and experience of those who will lead the effort in every grant proposal. This is crucial because . . .

> ➤ Knowing your strengths enables you to align your talents with grantor priorities: If a church or non-profit can show that its strengths align with the grantor's objectives and priorities, it increases the likelihood of receiving funding. For instance, if some people on your team have

experience in teaching, agencies that provide funding for tutoring are more likely to approve the application.

➤ Emphasizing an organization's unique strengths can set it apart from other applicants. Knowing your strengths builds confidence and gives you a competitive edge among others who are applying for the same funds. Agencies that fund programs to promote health and address specific health problems are looking for teams with one or more people with experience in healthcare.

➤ Understanding your personal and organizational strengths produces a clearer, more focused program design. This gets back to the need to clarify your vision. Don't be scattered. Don't try to do everything. Do what you can do with excellence and joy.

➤ Organizations that know how to play to their strengths are often more resilient and adaptable, giving them long-term viability, which results in continued funding. As you've seen from our stories, this has become the norm for our relationships with officials in a number of agencies. Local officials know Citi Church has experience and expertise in community engagement. That's who we are, and they trust us to provide outstanding services.

➤ Many grant relationships are long-term. Demonstrating strengths and proven results can lead to continued or increased funding in the future. Agency officials don't necessarily have strong relationships with all of us, but we want them to have a strong connection with at least one of us.

Some leaders take a tour of the Dream Center in Los Angeles and want to duplicate it. Big dreams are wonderful, but progress happens when leaders recognize the strengths of their team and use those talents to create maximum impact. Know yourself, know your team, and know your community . . . and design a plan that fits. When you know what you do well, you'll have confidence you can pull off programs you plan, and agencies are more easily convinced you'll be a valued partner.

Trust is the currency of strong relationships—all strong relationships.

In 2016, we applied for a three-year grant through the Department of Juvenile Justice. When the three years were over, the director called to tell us we were doing an amazing job, and he wanted to extend the contract to fund our program helping troubled young people turn their lives around. We still have the funding and a good relationship with the department today, long after the initial three-year term ended. Trust is the currency of strong relationships—all strong relationships.

THE HERO OF THE STORY

The backstory of the drama of David and Goliath is that when Samuel went to Jesse's house to anoint a new king and asked him to bring all his sons to him, Jesse didn't value David enough to include him among his sons. The boy was, in his father's eyes, the runt of the litter. Later, when David's brothers had joined King Saul's army to fight the Philistines, Jesse sent David on an errand to take bread and cheese to the brothers' captain and bring back a report of the fighting. When David arrived at the camp, he saw Saul's army march to the battlefield. David ran to see his brothers, and then he saw Goliath. He learned that Goliath had challenged Saul to send out one man to fight him, and the winner's army would make the loser's army their slaves. David's anger flared up, and he was incensed that no one was willing to fight the giant. Someone told Saul about David, and the king sent for him. When David arrived, he told Saul, "Don't worry about this Philistine. I'll go fight him!"

"Don't be ridiculous!" Saul replied. "There's no way you can fight this Philistine and possibly win! You're only a boy, and he's been a man of war since his youth."

But David persisted. "I have been taking care of my father's sheep and goats," he said. "When a lion or a bear comes to steal a lamb from the flock, I go after it with a club and rescue the lamb from its mouth. If the animal turns on me, I catch it by the jaw and club it to death. I have done this to both lions and bears, and I'll do it to this pagan Philistine, too, for he has defied the armies of the living God! The Lord who rescued me from the claws of the lion and the bear will rescue me from this Philistine!"

Saul saw no other volunteers, so he told the young man, "All right, go ahead," he said. "And may the Lord be with you!" Before David left, Saul gave him his armor: a bronze helmet and a coat of mail, but Saul was a tall man, so the armor didn't fit. David took it off, picked up his sling and five smooth stones, and walked into the valley.

You know the rest of the story: Goliath laughed and sneered at the seemingly unarmed boy who had come to fight him to the death, but David replied,

> *You come to me with sword, spear, and javelin, but I come to you in the name of the Lord of Heaven's Armies—the God of the armies of Israel, whom you have defied. Today the Lord will conquer you, and I will kill you and cut off your head. And then I will give the dead bodies of your men to the birds and wild animals, and the whole world will know that there is a God in Israel! And everyone assembled here will know that the Lord rescues his people, but not with sword and spear. This is the Lord's battle, and he will give you to us!—1 Samuel 17:32-51*

As Goliath and David moved toward each other, David took out a stone, put it in his sling, and hit Goliath in the forehead, killing him instantly. The Philistines turned and ran for their lives. It was one of the most stunning victories in all of history. How had it happened? Someone who had been overlooked had hidden skills (he had killed a lion and a bear), and even though no one else, including his father and his brothers, believed in him, David trusted God, took a huge risk, and stepped out in faith. He didn't rely on the strengths of others (Saul's armor); he relied on the talents and experiences God had given him. He put those into action at that pivotal moment, and the course of history was changed that day.

David was ready because God had orchestrated everything so he could rise to the challenge.

We need to remember that the hero of the story isn't David. The hero is God. He's the one who prepared David for that moment. Through years of rejection, ridicule, and loneliness, God honed his character and skills to be ready for that moment. David was ready because God had orchestrated everything so he could rise to the challenge.

God is the hero of our stories, too. He has taken each of us through hard times to strengthen our faith, and He has blessed us so we know the true source of our strength. When we look at ourselves, we may see a "runt," but God sees an overcomer. When we look back on our lives, we may see failure, but God sees valuable experiences. When we look at the challenges of today, we may hear words of "can't," "won't," and "don't," but God says, "When you're weak, I'm strong. Trust me."

NO SMALL THING

When we planted Citi Church, I (Dianna) dreamed of it becoming the next Hillsong. I believed we were going to take the city by storm! Not long after we started (maybe it was when ten people showed up the second Sunday!), God began to show me that my dream of something magnificent was more about me than about Him. I realized that becoming a huge success had become an idol, capturing my attention and my heart. I was broken and surrendered to God in a new and important way. This was (and is) His church, not mine. The Lord put a phrase in my heart that still resonates today: *Every step of faith is no small thing.* Even when our church was very small, every conversation, every hug of comfort and word of affirmation, mattered . . . to the person I was talking to, to me, and to God. The kingdom of God will one day be enormous and glorious in the new heavens and new earth, but God's kingdom is built today brick by brick as we take small steps of faith-filled obedience to reach out and care for those around us.

Today, twenty years later, some very big churches are asking for our help in securing grant funding as their vision expands to match the needs of their communities. We are at this point today because we took thousands of small, often seemingly insignificant, and mundane steps, and God has blessed us.

When God told Moses to confront Pharaoh, he was terrified. Who was he to make demands of the most powerful ruler in the world, the one who had all the Israelites as slaves under his thumb? Moses argued with God, insisting he didn't have what it would take to convince either the slaves or Pharoah that God had actually sent him. Moses protested, "What if they won't believe me or listen to me? What if they say, 'The Lord never appeared to you'?"

Then the Lord asked him, "What is that in your hand?"

"A shepherd's staff," Moses replied.

"Throw it down on the ground," the Lord told him. So Moses threw down the staff, and it turned into a snake! Moses jumped back.

Then the Lord told him, "Reach out and grab its tail." So Moses reached out and grabbed it, and it turned back into a shepherd's staff in his hand.

"Perform this sign," the Lord told him. "Then they will believe that the Lord, the God of their ancestors—the God of Abraham, the God of Isaac, and the God of Jacob—really has appeared to you." (Exodus 4:1-5)

We believe that's what God is asking each of us: What's in your hand? What are the talents and experiences you have right now? An MBA might be helpful, or a doctorate in leadership or administration, but God has made you enough right now for the creative, heart-expanding, life-changing, consequential vision He has (or will) put on your heart.

Just say, "Yes!"

Pastors, get out your shovel and do the work to uncover hidden treasures in the people on your team. Staff members, notice what others do especially well and tell them what you see, especially as they're doing it. Don't be threatened by their excellence. Remember that you're God's masterpiece too!

THINK ABOUT IT:

1) Have you ever been surprised to find out someone you know has a hidden talent? What led to the discovery? How did it change your perception of that person?

2) What are some reasons we resist being in a place where we have no option but to take a risk to trust God?

3) What do you think Paul meant when he wrote, "For when I am weak, then I am strong"?

4) Review the points under "Related to Grants." Which of these inspires you? Which challenged you? How will you respond?

5) Why is it important to realize Jesus is the hero of our stories? What difference does that realization make?

6) Are you content to do "small things"? Why or why not?

CHAPTER 6

"DON'T MESS WITH GOD!"

I t was a "can't miss" idea. As construction on our building was coming to an end in 2005, we wanted to find ways to introduce ourselves to people in the neighborhood. One of us (we can't remember who had the brainstorm) thought about buying cases of blue-tin containers of Royal Dansk Danish Butter Cookies. Everybody loves them! I (Dianna) bought the cookies at a local Walgreens, and we carried them in big plastic containers with handles. Each tin was wrapped with a ribbon holding a flyer about Citi Church. We wanted to bless people, so we carried the tins and knocked on doors—we were full of God's power and passion! This was our first foray to connect with people we'd been praying for. Our excitement was off the charts!

At the first house, a woman barely cracked the door. When we began our introduction and explanation that the blue tin of cookies was a gift from our church, she didn't let us finish the first sentence. She slammed the door without a word.

Well, I thought, she's just having a bad day. We went to the next house. We could see people moving around inside, but no one came to the door. At another house, people peeked through the curtains to see who we were, but they didn't open the door. We wanted to yell, "Hello, we see you! We're not a threat. We just want to bless you today." They stared at us and our eyes locked, but the door was too. We knocked on dozens of doors that day, but only a few were willing to take a tin of cookies . . . and they looked at us like we were from another planet!

We went back to the church building so discouraged. We had lived in upstate South Carolina, where everyone spoke to each other, and a lot of people still didn't lock their houses at night. There, people treat strangers like friends. When you're filling your car with gas, you might have a twenty-minute conversation with someone you'd never seen before. Miami was culture shock. (It was like the Lord was speaking a take-off from *The Wizard of Oz*[13]: "You're not in South Carolina anymore!")

We were disheartened, disillusioned, and distraught. How could we build a church with people who wouldn't even talk to us? We knew we needed to debrief what had happened. We didn't have to go out for refreshments—we had plenty of cookies! In our conversation, we realized we didn't know our community. We didn't understand their hopes and fears, their suspicions, and their reasonable reluctance to interact with us. We later heard that Jehovah's Witness

---

13 Victor Fleming, *The Wizard of Oz* (August 25, 1939; Beverly Hills, CA: Metro-Goldwyn-Mayer Studios, Inc.).

teams regularly canvassed the neighborhood, so maybe they assumed we were with them. As immigrants from Central and South America, most of the people were from a Catholic background. We didn't fit in that category for them. A lot of houses had bars on the windows. We hadn't paid much attention to this fact before, but now we understood that self-protection was important—and necessary—to them. But we also realized another fact: They didn't know us. They didn't realize we meant them no harm, and we wanted to reach out to them as friends. We had a lot of work to do to build trust with our community.

Over the next few weeks, we noticed something striking: No matter how poor a family might be, when they had virtually any kind of celebration, they rented a bounce house. Our observation became a strategy: We hosted a lot of carnivals in our parking lot, and of course, they featured several bounce houses—some like the original ones where kids jumped on inflated platforms, and some were tall slides and mini waterparks.

"GETTING TO KNOW YOU"

We found several valuable resources to help us understand our part of Miami.

Demographics

Melissa Data (https://www.melissa.com/) provides a wealth of information, including mailing addresses. Also, the Census Bureau has all kinds of data about each community.

It's important to remember that demographics can shift. For instance, a church in a sleepy country town twenty miles from a city can find that the city has expanded to include them. The audience for their church then includes individuals and families who commute, make a lot more money than the average income in the town before the influx of new people, and are used to the amenities and pace of city life. If the formerly country church doesn't realize this shift, the leaders may not take advantage of the new opportunities to reach the new neighbors. In our experience, marginalized communities still prefer information to be written and handed or mailed to them, but people in upscale areas pay more attention to ads on social media.

Felt needs

To get on the same wavelength with people around us, we needed a tool to help us discover their genuine concerns. Christian Community Development Association (www.ccda. org) helps churches engage more effectively with their communities. We used a simple survey to ask open-ended questions, and the feedback was very clear—people wanted more resources for their kids and grandkids. They felt their children were falling behind, and they were well aware of the potential consequences of drugs, crime, and violence.

We never stopped asking questions. The answers from a lot of people may be similar, but each new person we ask feels valued, heard, and understood. As political movements push different buttons on policies of immigration, the economy, sex ethics, and other volatile issues, staying engaged with people lets them know we understand the sources of their anxiety.

Existing champions

It's important to identify organizations that are already having an impact on the community. We're not there to compete with them. It's far healthier and more effective to partner with them. When we were connected with Family & Children Faith Coalition, we didn't try to duplicate their programs; instead, we became one of their programs. Yvonne Sawyer put us in touch with the Christian Community Development Association so we could have more tools to reach our neighborhood.

Sometimes people ask us to provide clothes. We don't have that service, but we don't just shrug and say, "Sorry." We can point them to several organizations to meet this need. When a food bank, a clothing resource, or an organization that provides housing, mental health care, tutoring, assistance for parents, or any other local service learns that we've referred people to them, they naturally refer people to us if we can help. That's how we organically build strong partnerships. For instance, a private school in a more affluent part of the city that isn't far away sometimes refers students to our school, especially if the student has proven to be difficult to manage and lives near our neighborhood.

High-level connections

To become a force for good in a community, church leaders need to get to know the local leaders. Ask for appointments to meet the mayor, city council members, school principals, hospital administrators, and business leaders. At a minimum, they'll know who you are so they can say positive things when your church is mentioned in conversations, and from time to time, you'll need them to help with a sticky problem, such as zoning, security, or a misunderstanding with the police department.

TRY THESE . . .

We were so eager to relate to people in our area that we tried all kinds of approaches. Here are a few:

Prayer Walks

Many times, we walked around the neighborhood praying for the people in each home. If someone was outside, we stopped to talk (if they didn't run inside!). On a few occasions, we discovered things we'd never imagined before. We encountered Santeros, priests of an African diasporic religion called Santeria that developed in Cuba. They dress in white and put curses on people. In our prayer walks, we discovered that many in our community were open to this kind of spiritualism. This isn't just a benign hobby. The leaders are powerbrokers who demand large payments, or they'll put a curse that will cause the person to die—or at least, that's their threat. We may think that's ridiculous, but a lot of people believe it . . . and pay for protection. When our church opened, and it became known that we were preaching the gospel of Jesus, we often found dead chickens, bags of chicken guts, and statues of saints on our property to curse us. They knew the power of the gospel was breaking strongholds, and this was their way of fighting back. At one point, they climbed our fence, erected a saint on the front door, and made sacrifices to it.

Another problem that alarmed us in the early years was theft. We experienced break-ins fairly often. At the time, Dianna and I (Tony) hadn't found storage for a lot of the things we'd brought from South Carolina, so we kept them in a room at the church. One morning, I walked in to find that my collection of New York Yankees memorabilia was gone. I was really angry. As I prayed, I sensed the Lord ask me, "Are you more concerned about the memorabilia you lost or the people in your community who are lost?" Ouch!

> **For us, the prayer walks were both spiritual and practical—we asked God to work in people's lives, and we used interactions to tell people about our church and invite them to come.**

Prayer walks were an important part of getting acquainted with our neighbors—often in ways that built trust, but sometimes in more threatening ways. Walking through a neighborhood gives you a very different perspective than driving around. When you walk, you notice details you wouldn't have picked up any other way. Walking lets you smell as well as see—dinner on the stove, fumes from engines, animals in the yard, marijuana, and other odors that provide another layer of understanding the people. Gradually, the Holy Spirit reveals things. On a particular walk, I (Dianna) remember feeling the need to stop and pray for the people in a particular house. The Lord led us to pray against addiction and abuse and for hope and healing. We got a map of the community from the local library, and we used it to make sure we made prayer walks on every street. When we came back, we marked that we'd been on that street, and we talked about what we saw, heard, smelled, and sensed from the Lord as we walked.

Years ago, our pastor, the late Bishop Tony Miller, taught that Jesus went from a prayer meeting in the morning to a prayer meeting at night, and in between, He performed miracles. That was our perspective, too. We walked and prayed, and when we encountered people with a need, we trusted God to meet it. For us, the prayer walks were both spiritual and practical—we asked God to work in people's lives, and we used interactions to tell people about our church and invite them to come.

Knocking on Doors

Our attempt to give away cookies had been, well, not a complete disaster, but not very productive either. That changed when Hurricane Wilma roared through the city. When we knocked on doors to give out sandwiches, people eagerly met us, received our gifts, and thanked us for caring.

One year, we prepared Thanksgiving baskets of food for people who weren't part of our church. A few new believers in our group went to a house where a lady came to the door and looked like she was high on drugs. Behind her was an older woman dressed as a Voodoo witch doctor. They were scared. I (Tony) think they felt like the sons of Sceva when an evil spirit confronted them:

"Jesus I know, and Paul I know about, but who are you?" (Acts 19:15, NIV). The new believers called me to come over and see this sight. When I arrived, I asked the lady if I could come in and pray for them, and to my surprise, she let me in. When I prayed, I sensed a spiritual breakthrough in their hearts. Their countenance changed: Instead of the presence of evil, we saw the presence of joy. It was a Thanksgiving I'll never forget.

A few days before Christmas one year, someone donated a lot of live Christmas trees to us and asked us to give them away. We sent teams door to door to bless people. In one house, the parents were thrilled to have a tree because they couldn't afford one, and their son was mesmerized by the sight of it. They came to church that Sunday for the first time, and they became faithful members.

Community Events

As we mentioned, from the earliest days of the church, we hosted carnivals in our parking lot with bounce houses, hot dogs, popcorn, drinks, and all kinds of games for kids and adults. We gave each person tickets to activities and concessions so they'd make the rounds and make sure no one took so much that others had nothing. We played music, so it was a full-on block party. In those days, we didn't have enough volunteers to pull off these events, but two other churches, Miami Harvest Center and New Harvest Church, sent people to serve with us. At the time, my (Dianna) parents, Ben and Elma Williams, lived in Clewiston, Florida, about an hour and a half away, and they came to support us. My dad owned a Hawaiian Shaved Ice stand, and he set it up to serve our community. As former missionaries, they were excited to be a part of helping us reach out to the community. Our first carnival drew about 500 people, and they grew larger each time.

People have asked how a church plant could afford events this big and elaborate. The answer is that the Lord provided. For the first one, a man who attended another church heard about us and offered to pay all the expenses, and for others, generous people graciously paid for all or most of the cost.

At one of the early community carnivals, a man showed up with a gun. He had been involved in domestic abuse, and he came to the event with violence on his mind. I (Tony) asked someone to call the police, and they came quickly to arrest him. That gives you an idea of what was going on in our part of the city.

At the same event, we had a lot of new believers who served in every capacity, including security. We had about ten bounce houses—a couple of them were two stories tall—and kids were waiting in line for each one. What a day! But in the middle of the event, one of the bounce houses lost its air and was flat on the ground. Of course, each of them is powered by an engine that continually blows air. A couple of our young men who were serving as security saw that the generator was gone. We'd given our guys walkie-talkies so we could stay connected if there was a problem—and now we had one! One of them glanced down the sidewalk and saw a guy pulling the generator! One of our guys yelled, "Pastor, we're gonna get him!" He and another of our guys ran after him, tackled him, and pulled his pants down around his feet so he couldn't jump up and run off. As I ran to them, I called the police. The walkie-talkies were on, and I heard one of our guys growling at the thief, "That's what happens when you mess with God!"

We learned a valuable lesson in the early days of Citi Church. When we went out into the community to meet people and build relationships, we encountered resistance, but when we hosted these fun, family-friendly events, people came in droves. They got to see us and know us, and they began to trust us.

On a few occasions, we combined a health fair with carnivals. A couple of our members, Faith Bailey and Stephanie McNeil, were instrumental in organizing the health fair. Inside the church, we had booths set up by several healthcare providers. People came inside and received free services such as readings for blood pressure and cholesterol levels, vision screening, and safe sex with free condoms. (We asked them to remove the condoms because we didn't want to be known for promoting sex, but we still allowed them to participate in the event.) At each booth, cards were stamped, which gave people credits for food and events outside. The organizations that participated with us became partners. They needed to meet a quota for funding, but they had limited access to the community. That changed when they joined us in our carnivals. They easily exceeded their quotas in one day. From then on, we could refer people to them when we discovered a need, and they sent people to us when we could minister to them as pastors or with one of our community service programs.

Two local banks also wanted to partner with us at these events. They knew that underserved and marginalized people often needed banking services but were afraid to trust large institutions with their money. The banks set up booths and informed people how to set up accounts and use debit cards. This partnership created a way for the banks to come to the people in our community instead of people having to go to them.

School Outreaches

One of our first strategies to get involved in the community was "adopting" Comstock Elementary and becoming the principal's partner. Our emphasis was serving the teachers. We offered to provide a back-to-school breakfast for them. Starbucks gave us coffee, Dunkin' Donuts provided boxes of sweets, and Panera Bread sent breakfast sandwiches. As we mentioned earlier, we put tablecloths and fresh flowers on the tables, and we had everything set up before the first teacher arrived. We wore our Citi Church shirts so they'd know who we were. We eventually expanded this outreach to teachers to five more schools. We served them four times a year, which is a total of twenty-four. We served breakfast a couple of times a year, and we had smaller events for Christmas and the end of the school year. For these, we wrapped small gifts that included a thank-you note for caring for their students.

Before the administrators knew us and trusted us, they insisted on us giving them the gifts so they could put them in the mailboxes. When they got to know us, they let us put the gifts in the teachers mailboxes. Later, as the relationships blossomed, they allowed us to put church flyers for the students (to promote events like our carnivals and other events) in the teachers' mailboxes so they could distribute them to the students in our community.

In our involvement with schools, we discovered two people who can smooth the way or put up roadblocks: the front desk receptionist and the custodian. The receptionist is the gate-keeper who allows (or doesn't allow) communication to flow to the administration, teachers, and students. For every event at the school, we depend on custodians to open doors, set up rooms, and provide other services for us. When you treat them with love and respect, and when you show appreciation for them in tangible ways, they open doors . . . literally and figuratively.

We've mentioned that we participated in backpack give-aways. One year, at the beginning of the school year, we used our church service to give backpacks to students, and of course, many parents came with their kids. Late August is hot in Miami, and people had to wait in a long line with their children. We rushed to get cold water to them. We had 800 backpacks ready to go . . . but 1,200 children showed up! That's a problem! We gave 400 rainchecks so we could scramble to get more to give them the next Sunday. We had to use our church's American Express card to buy more that week. It was a bit chaotic, but it was a good problem when so many families count on our church as a valued resource.

Later, the city picked up the torch to provide backpacks, and we became their partner.

Keep Your Ear to the Ground

From time to time, we find out about new organizations that can partner with us. For instance, we recently discovered a group called Branches, which raises money for supplies and cooks Thanksgiving feasts to distribute to those who can't afford a lavish family banquet for the holiday. They do it all: raising funds, shopping, cooking, packaging, and delivery. They asked for our help to identify needy families. We gave them 170 names and addresses of those we regularly serve, and Branches took it from there.

A good reputation draws interest, compassion, and resources.

We also have a community Thanksgiving celebration every year where people come to enjoy being together and have a nice dinner. Recently, a generous couple offered to pay for everything: pumpkins, decorations, food, and a bounce house for kids. We didn't contact them. When they heard about our ministry to people in the inner city, they wanted to get involved, and they reached out to us. We'd never met them, but someone told someone who told someone who told them, and their hearts were moved to make the day extra special. A good reputation draws interest, compassion, and resources. In Proverbs 22:1 (NKJV), Solomon explained, "A good name is to be chosen rather than great riches, loving favor rather than silver and gold."

Attend Civic Gatherings

It's important to network with community leaders, agency directors, and pastors at events like city council meetings to meet and greet. In the early years of our church, the mayor held an event in the first week of December to light the Christmas tree for the city of Miami, and he told his staff, "We need a reverend to pray."

One of them responded, "Pastor Tony has been at all our meetings. Let's ask him."

Citi Church was young and small. They could have found the pastor of one of the megachurches in the city, but since they knew me, they asked me to participate. That night, I sat next to the mayor before I was introduced and prayed. In the audience, I saw several leading pastors. The look on their faces said, "Who is that guy? And what's he doing on the platform with the mayor?" From the earliest days, we've practiced "the ministry of showing up." We go to city council meetings, planning and zoning meetings, and virtually any other civic gathering and we encourage you to do the same.

Participate in Community Events

In addition to meetings held by the mayor, city council, and other government agencies, "**the ministry of showing up**" applies to a wide range of other activities, such as high school sports, prayer breakfasts, concerts, plays, and other events sponsored by schools, churches, and community groups. Even brief, casual conversations can lead to much bigger partnerships. For instance, the director of Young Dreams, a local organization supporting children for educational success, shows up at many of our events, and we partner together at many of hers. Even if not a single dollar or a moment of volunteering passes between us, we feel supported by one another—and in the nonprofit world, that's really important.

In many communities, high school football games in the fall are the most important community events of the year. Do you want to rub shoulders with people from all walks of life? Go to high school sporting events. You'll meet the whole city there.

Service Projects

The heart of the gospel is Christ's sacrifice for those who don't deserve it. That's what captured our hearts the day we trusted in Him, and that's what animates and directs our lives today. We can be the hands and feet of Jesus by serving faithfully, diligently, and joyfully in mundane tasks for the sake of the city. We've participated in community clean-up days, "adopt a highway," distributing packages of resources to the homeless, and similar outreaches. We try to make it easy for people to participate. We list the opportunities on our website and explain how to get involved. And again, we collaborate with other churches and organizations for virtually all these efforts.

I'd suggest that one of the most fruitful activities is to lay our assumptions and biases aside and learn to look at people around us with fresh eyes and an open heart.

LESSON LEARNED

Some of us have come to our present communities from the outside, so we had to do the work to know what's going on in our neighborhoods. But others are serving where they were born and raised, or at least they've lived there long enough to feel like natives. Our advice for all of us is to be an explorer, to look at our communities with fresh eyes, to ask penetrating questions, and to be open to having our perspectives challenged. We are creatures of habit, not just of the body but also of the mind. That means we have baked-in social, racial, and political biases, and they're so familiar that we don't even recognize them. If we don't take time to look more deeply into the hearts and lives of people inside and outside our churches, we'll give them what we think they need instead of what they actually need.

I (Tony) know this involves a lot of work. Many church leaders are overwhelmed with the responsibility to lead sheep who are prone to wander off, fight with each other, and resist when we gently prod them with our staff. We all have a finite amount of time, and I'd suggest that one of the most fruitful activities is to lay our assumptions and biases aside and learn to look at people around us with fresh eyes and an open heart.

Thirty years ago, when I was a middle school teacher, I learned a valuable lesson. Virtually every student in my classroom had a juvenile record, so they weren't exactly the most compliant bunch you've ever seen. One of them was a real handful—defiant and resistant. I tried everything to connect with him, but nothing worked . . . until I went to his home. I knocked on the door, but it wasn't completely shut, and it slowly opened. I looked inside and saw a number of people passed out. I stepped in and called the student's name. He came down the stairs, saw me, and motioned for me to go back upstairs with him. He led me into a room with nothing on the walls and a bare mattress on the floor with pee stains and a pile of clothes. He sniffed them to see which shirt had the least offensive smell so he could put it on to talk with me. I put my arm around him and walked him down the street to get some ice cream.

I didn't have to ask any questions. A few moments in his environment told me all I needed to know about him and his responses to authority. From that moment, I gave him great grace. A few days after I went to his house, I asked, "Is this why you're so tired every day?" He nodded. "You need some sleep, don't you?" He nodded again. I told him, "When you come in each morning, you can get some sleep on the sofa in the back of the room." Every day, he slept for an hour and a half at the beginning of the school day, and after that, he participated in class. He was eager to learn, and he passed every course. Was he a different person because he got some sleep or because he felt my understanding, compassion, and support? Both, I'm sure. Going to his home to meet him in his environment and on his terms changed both of our lives. He trusted me, and I learned to look beneath the surface to see the person, not just the problem.

When you look at what's going on in your city, do you primarily see the problems of addiction, divorce, disease, abuse, unresolved conflict, and the deep cesspool of hurt, fear, anger, and shame that seems to have no end? Or, can you look a layer or two deeper to see broken hearts and shattered dreams? If all we see are problems, we're either overwhelmed, find ways to distance ourselves, or are compelled to fix the problems only so we feel better about ourselves. We need to remember that Jesus stepped out of heaven to join us on earth—He became one of us to share our sorrows and be acquainted with our griefs. His understanding of our problems broke His heart, and He sacrificed Himself to give us hope. This is how Augustine described Jesus sixteen centuries ago:

> *Man's maker was made man that He, Ruler of the stars, might nurse at His mother's breast; that the Bread might hunger, the Fountain thirst, the Light sleep, the Way be tired on His journey; that the Truth*

*might be accused of false witness, the Teacher be
beaten with whips, the Foundation be suspended
on wood; that Strength might grow weak; that the
Healer might be wounded; that Life might die.*[14]

That's the irony, isn't it? The creator of all became a baby;
the omnipotent one let Himself be murdered; the author of life
died that we might live. But thankfully, that wasn't the end of
the story. The resurrection of Jesus gives hope to the hopeless
and joy to the discouraged. His love and power conquer all!

When we make assumptions about people, they feel like
objects, but when we take time to be with them and understand them, they feel seen. When they feel seen, they feel
loved. It makes all the difference in a life, in a family, in a
church, and in a community.

---

14 St. Augustine, Sermons 191.1

THINK ABOUT IT:

1) When was the last time you looked at the up-to-date demographics of your community? How might it help you to look again to see what's changed?

2) What are the advantages of making assumptions about the felt needs of people around you? What are the downsides of these assumptions?

3) What are some specific ways you can become more in touch with the hopes and dreams of others in your city?

4) List the organizations that are actively serving near you. What ones could be good partners? What's your first step to make that connection?

5) Look at the list under "Try These . . ." Which ones are you currently doing? What impact are they having? Which ones could be very effective for you and your community?

6) Write a sentence or two of appreciation to Jesus for getting involved in our community of humankind.

CHAPTER 7

RIGHT PEOPLE, RIGHT ROLES

O ur success at Citi Church is due to the team God put together. We each bring different gifts and experiences. It's not too much to say that we're a microcosm of the body of Christ, "joined and held together by every supporting ligament, grows and builds itself up in love, as each part does its work" (Ephesians 4:16, NIV).

If you look at the people on your team and your key volunteers, do you see them as a unified, world-changing body of passionate and talented believers, or do you shake your head and wonder if you can do anything significant with those people? If you doubt your people (and perhaps yourself), take a look again at the ragtag bunch of David and his "mighty men." At first glance, the only thing mighty about them was their reputation as outcasts and outlaws—they were mighty messed up!

After David killed Goliath, the people were exultant and gave him the credit for the amazing victory over the Philistines.

But one person wasn't so thrilled . . . King Saul. He was jealous of the kid's popularity, and he was determined to eliminate him. Jonathan, Saul's son, tried to protect his friend, but all he could do was warn David to flee. The historian tells us,

> *So David left Gath and escaped to the cave of Adullam. Soon his brothers and all his other relatives joined him there. Then others began coming—men who were in trouble or in debt or who were just discontented—until David was the captain of about 400 men.—1 Samuel 22:1-2*

Let's read between the lines: They were "in trouble." What kind of trouble causes a man to flee for his life? It must have been big trouble! They were "in debt." We can assume they couldn't or wouldn't repay loans or make good on possessions they'd taken from others. They were "discontented." They saw themselves as victims of the system, and life wasn't fair. In other words, they complained a lot! And there were 400 of these misfits!

What did they see in David that attracted them to join him as a fugitive in a cave? It wasn't exactly the Ritz Carlton! What turned them from malcontents into David's "special forces"? David took them as they were, but he inspired them to be better than they ever thought possible. Together, this band, led by "the three" and "the thirty," fought when they had to and ran when the odds were against them. They became a legendary fighting force.

What does that have to do with how our teams can function? All of us were in trouble because our sinful nature condemned us to eternal judgment; we were in debt to God because our sins created an insurmountable deficit, and we were discontented in our selfishness, self-righteousness, and self-pity. But Jesus didn't leave us in our predicament. He called us, we answered, and since that day, He's been turning us into His special forces—equipped with the Spirit of God and the Word of God and trained by those among the people of God who are skilled and brave. We come to Jesus with nothing in our hands, but by His Spirit, He puts talents, experiences, and heart into us so we can play our part in expanding His kingdom.

Leaders need to create an environment that has a powerful blend of administration and pastoring.

In much of the Western world, people rely on classes to teach virtually every topic. This kind of instruction is fine, but only if it's coupled with experience. Jesus invited the disciples, "Follow me." He didn't say, "Sign up for my coursework." Following Him, watching, asking questions, and stepping out to put what we've seen into practice . . . that's how lives are transformed. The late Bishop Tony Miller, my (Tony's) pastor, invited me to join him in all kinds of activities, mundane and magnificent. When he was going to the hospital to visit someone, he often said, "Tony, come with me." When someone called to ask him to come and pray, he took several of us with him. On the way back, he invariably asked, "What did you see?" "What stood out to you?" "Why do you think I said or did this or that?" Then he sent us out two by two to minister like we'd seen him do in the prison, the hospital, the nursing home, the neighborhood. We came back full of more questions. Debriefing sessions, with honest feedback, were our primary classrooms. That's how Jesus trained his disciples, and it's still the most effective way today.

Leaders need to create an environment that has a powerful blend of administration and pastoring. If it's all administration, the team lacks life, heart, and hope; if it's all pastoring, there's little planning, order, or excellence. People on our teams need both—not one and then the other, but both at the same time . . . and continually. At Citi Church, if we lean a little more in one direction, it's toward pastoring. We often say, "People are more important than projects."

A HARD LESSON

Years ago, we hosted a conference at our church to celebrate the anniversary of the day our church was planted, and we had some renowned guest speakers. Our team worked hard to pull it off with excellence, and everyone gave it their all. We served meals to the out-of-town guests, and we worked into the nights to be sure every detail had been addressed. It was spectacularly successful. The Lord worked in amazing ways, but when it was over, our team was a trainwreck. We were nit-picking each other's performance, complaining about this or that, and either "getting big" by being loud and condemning or "getting little" by shrinking into silence to avoid any blow-back. I (Keisha) remember, "Everything looked good on the surface, but behind the scenes, we had chaos and anger. It was hypocritical to sing about God's love and teach about God's grace while the people running the show were at each other's throats! I didn't want to be a part of anything like that. Is this what Citi Church is going to be about? If it is, I'm out. I was ready to pack up and drive back to South Carolina. I'm out of here. This isn't for me."

I (Tony) had to swallow a bitter pill. I asked everyone to be honest about their feelings and perceptions, and they vented. It was painful but necessary. For the next month or two, we had to rebuild our fractured relationships. So, was the con-ference a success? Yes, but at a very high price, one that we determined never to pay again. We had valued performance over the people, and it caused a world of hurt. Keisha, Dianna, and I had been involved in churches that held big events like this fairly regularly, and I thought we could just duplicate the effort and the excellence. I quickly realized my assumption was very wrong.

We certainly have had many more events since then, but I've made a commitment to value the health of our team first. I realized I'd been exploiting the people on our team and the volunteers who had served so faithfully at the event. Is the word "exploit" too harsh? I don't think so. As the shep-herd, I was responsible to feed and protect the sheep, but I'd failed. I had been more committed to excellence (and impressing the guest speakers with our excellence) than cre-ating a supportive culture so people could serve with joy. The people on our team are my priority. Yes, we're doing a lot in inner-city Miami, and it takes work to administrate our many programs, but my role, first and foremost, is to care for the people on our team.

A church leader heard our story and our renewed commitment to blend administration and pastoring as we pursue grants to fund our outreaches, and he said, "But isn't what you're doing ninety-five percent administration and five percent pastoring?"

I (Keisha) responded, "It may look like that on the outside because you see grant proposals and programs being planned and executed but woven through all of this is our heart for people, including each other. When we work on a new project or fine-tune an existing one, I tell our staff and volunteers, 'We're in the people business.' We're not working on an assembly line. We're touching people at their point of need, and we're representing Jesus in all His love and power. If the people we're trying to serve and the people we are serving with don't feel loved, welcomed, and honored, then all our efforts will be for nothing."

GIVE 'EM THE PICKLE

Years ago, I (Tony) read a book called *Give 'Em the Pickle* by Robert Farrell. (Yes, I know that sounds really strange, but stay with me.) He owned a restaurant that specialized in hamburgers. One day, he got a letter from one of his regular customers. The letter began with high praise for the quality of the hamburgers she enjoyed, and she explained that when she asked for an extra pickle, she always got one. But the most recent time she was in the restaurant and asked for an extra pickle, the manager told her, "We don't give free extra pickle slices any longer, but you can have one for seventy-five cents." The writer expressed her disappointment. She concluded, "Because of that, I'm not going to your restaurant any longer."

Farrell didn't know about the new pickle policy, and he was alarmed. He gathered his staff and told them, "If someone asks for a pickle, give 'em the pickle! We're creating an experience for people to enjoy."[15]

After I read this story, I brought a jar of pickles to our team meeting, told them about the letter Robert Farrell had received and his response to his staff, and I told our team, "When people ask for a pickle, give 'em the pickle!"

I (Dianna) want people to know that Tony is always on the people side of the equation. He gives extra grace, an abundance of mercy, and a second chance (or two or three). When things become too bureaucratic, he turns strange colors! But Tony values people who are on the other end, those like Keisha and me whose gifts are more in details, order, and execution. We've had to tell him that sometimes people aren't just taking one extra pickle, they're taking the whole jar. They're taking advantage of his generous nature. When we make him aware of these moments, he's willing to pull back the reins a bit with those people and say the words he really doesn't ever like to say, "You've had enough." For this to happen, everyone on the team has to be given an honored place so their voice is valued. We don't have to agree with each other, but we need to listen well, ask follow-up questions, and try to understand

---

15 Robert E. Farrell, *Give 'Em the Pickle* (Legacy Communications, 1998).

their point of view so we can express it as well as they do. When that happens, people know you know what they know.

THE RIGHT PEOPLE

Some leaders hire or build their teams too quickly. They don't do their due diligence to carefully evaluate applicants or get to know people, which sometimes (often!) results in having team members who don't fit the culture . . . and we have learned this the HARD way.

One way to know if the people on your team pass the chemistry test is your reaction the moment you drive into the parking lot and see their car.

At Citi Church, we've learned to look for people who have capacity, calling, character, and chemistry: the ability to do what we need them to do, a sense of God's leading, the integrity to do the right thing when no one is looking, and a relational fit with others on the team.

One way to know if the people on your team pass the chemistry test is your reaction the moment you drive into the parking lot and see their car. If knowing they're in the office makes you think, *Great! I'm looking forward to seeing that person today!* it's a good sign. But if you think, *Oh man, another long day,* the right chemistry isn't there.

THE IMPORTANCE OF CULTURE

This doesn't mean that everyone thinks, feels, and acts alike. Strong teams are built on honest give and take. When people can disagree without contempt, trust grows. Different perspectives often threaten insecure leaders, but good leaders know that a fresh set of eyes is often very valuable. Diversity is a strength, but only if each person—and each person's unique contribution—is valued. Do you think people on a team know how gossip, blame, and image management can be corrosive? Of course, they do, but if that's the culture, they learn to live with it, playing games with the truth, withholding credit, finding fault, and creating competing alliances. On our team, we teach Patrick Lencioni's *Five Dysfunctions of a Team,*[16] so issues of trust and respect are front and center in our relationships. Avoiding conflict doesn't build trust but addressing it with courage and tact certainly will. Teamwork requires accountability. Each person has an important role to play, but success is a shared experience.

If you want to solicit grant funding for community outreach programs, the culture of your team is your greatest asset (or a painful liability). Elements of a dynamic, positive culture can certainly be written down, but what we practice is far more powerful than words on a page. It starts with the leader building relationships of trust in meeting after

---

16 Patrick Lencioni, *The Five Dysfunctions of a Team: A Leadership Fable* (San Francisco, CA: Jossey-Bass, 2022).

meeting, conversation after conversation, and event after event. A secure leader welcomes different points of view but then knows when and how to decide to move forward. When people feel heard, they're far more likely to support a decision they wouldn't have made. When people feel marginalized or not heard, seeds of distrust and resentment often sprout, grow, and choke out whatever is good in the team's culture. People who don't feel valued may respond in several different ways: Some become defiant, others try to prove themselves and their value by pointing to their success; still, others try desperately to please the leader to win approval, and some hide in their offices or in plain sight to avoid any hint of conflict. These are signs of a person, and perhaps a culture, that needs attention.

When we planted Citi Church, I (Dianna) didn't know myself very well at all. I assumed my way of perceiving, thinking, speaking, and acting was just fine, but then, why were there so many misunderstandings? Why such tension? For a long time, I was sure the problem was them, but God showed me that the first person who needed inner transformation was me. A great team isn't one where I'm calling the shots and putting down those who disagree with me. At one point, I was frustrated when I found out people weren't being honest with me. Others took me aside and let me know what this person or that person thought about me or their questions about something I said or did. I wondered, Why don't they tell me? What am I doing that's creating a barrier? Why are they afraid to be honest with me? I tried to tell myself it was the fact that I was a pastor and they had problems with authority, but this deflection didn't answer all the questions. I had to face the fact that they were responding to times when I was too blunt, I didn't listen, my facial expressions communicated disapproval, and they didn't feel that I cared for them. No wonder they didn't feel they could be open and honest with me! I had been a chief reason for dysfunction on our team. Thankfully, God revealed this to me, and He softened my heart so I began to value others' opinions.

In his book *Emotionally Healthy Spirituality,* Peter Scazzero observes, "When genuine love is released in relationship, God's presence is manifest. The separate space between us becomes sacred space."[17] This concept changed me and changed my relationships—every moment with people is precious because they are precious.

THE LEARNING CURVE

Futurist and author Alvin Toffler taught that to grow, we need to learn, unlearn, and relearn. This is the model of discipleship, too. We come to Christ with a set of beliefs and perceptions. We've learned them from past experiences, but Paul teaches us that as we follow Christ, we have to unlearn and relearn:

> *You were taught, with regard to your former way of life, to put off your old self, which is being corrupted by its deceitful desires; to be made new in the attitude of your minds; and to put on the new self, created*

---

17 Peter Scazzero, *Emotionally Healthy Spirituality: It's Impossible to Be Spiritually Mature, While Remaining Emotionally Immature* (Grand Rapids, MI: Zondervan, 2017).

to be like God in true righteousness and holiness.
—Ephesians 4:22-24 (NIV)

He compared our volitional choices to changing clothes: We had old clothes on, but we take those off (that's unlearning) and put on clothes of the new self, beautiful clothes of kindness, love, righteousness, and purity. The context of this passage is Paul's explanation of the body of Christ. We can't unlearn and relearn on our own. It takes "iron sharpening iron" of rich, honest, supportive relationships.

When I (Keisha) joined Pastor Tony and Pastor Dianna in this crazy venture of planting Citi Church, each of us brought a measure of wisdom from our previous experiences. As we launched into grant funding for community outreaches, we grew with the opportunities. We gained new skills and sharpened existing ones, so we had greater capacity to plan and manage bigger programs. Our sense of calling never wavered, but it became more focused as we saw God use particular efforts, which reinforced our commitment to be more effective. As Pastor Tony described, at one point our team chemistry needed some serious attention, but instead of ignoring the problem, he led us in a process of self-discovery, repentance, and restoration.

It's perfectly fine to start where you are. Identify what each person on the team brings to the table, take steps forward to learn more about the specific needs in your neighborhood, find organizations that might partner with you, plan programs, pursue funding from government agencies, and see what God will do. As you come together around a common vision, you'll undoubtedly discover some previously hidden talents, you'll face new obstacles that challenge you to learn and grow, and you'll develop the two essential traits: a compassionate heart and fierce tenacity.

Don't be afraid to ride the learning curve. That's how individuals, teams, and organizations grow. Learn to live with some questions not yet answered. Some people are very comfortable with ambiguity, but others aren't. Know that, and for those who aren't, provide assurances that you don't have to have all the answers before you take steps forward.

LET PEOPLE RESPOND AT THEIR OWN PACE

When we've talked to leaders and teams about using grant funding for outreaches, we've gotten a wide range of reactions. Entrepreneurs are instantly excited and want to get going, many need more information before they get on board, and a few are resistant because the concept simply doesn't fit in their box. This range of responses is entirely normal. Initial reluctance isn't a sin or a sign of a lack of faith. It just means some people are slower to make commitments. Be patient and persistent. Do what it takes to give them a taste of the payoff for this kind of effort.

One of the lessons we learned is that we needed to create a team within our team. The three of us are the core team for grant writing and planning. Others on our team have their hands full with their ministry responsibilities, and we don't need everyone to participate in the grant writing process. But when we get a grant, for instance, for an after-school program, our youth and children's ministries get involved in making it happen. We dovetail every outreach program with an existing ministry (or two or three) in the church.

A few people on our team have backgrounds and talents in writing and editing, so we ask them to proof our grant proposals and give us feedback. We want each proposal to be crystal clear, thorough, and error-free, and these people help to make that happen. When they read about a new way to reach people in the community, they get excited, so we have another person who catches the vision and spreads it to others.

We learned something else at the beginning. At first, we shared information freely with everybody on the team, but some people were freaked out when something didn't go perfectly, so we began to tailor our communication more carefully. Our core team is completely transparent with each other, but we share more selectively with the rest of our team. This isn't dishonest; it's being wise to discern who can handle what information.

When people in the congregation get excited and share the vision with others, it's amazing how they pay attention, catch fire, and spread the vision to more people.

Actually, some of the most important people in our outreach vision aren't on our team. They're members of our church who may sit on the back row but have a lot of influence on others in the church. We learned that it's important to identify those who are highly respected and whose opinion carries a lot of weight. We cast vision with them at the same level as we cast it with our team. When people in the congregation get excited and share the vision with others, it's amazing how they pay attention, catch fire, and spread the vision to more people.

The Bible is full of stories about flawed but courageous people who stepped out of their comfort zones to do something great for God and his kingdom. Nehemiah had a comfortable career, but he left it to lead a complex construction effort. Esther risked her life to defend the Jews and save God's people from extermination. Abraham, Moses, Joshua, Gideon, Deborah, and the rest of the heroes listed in Hebrews 11 were captured by a vision to make a difference in their times. Has God given you a vision that inspires you to reach people and advance the kingdom in your time?

Of course, He has.

THINK ABOUT IT:

1) What kind of leader did David have to be to turn a bunch of outcasts into special forces? How do these leadership principles apply to you and your team?

2) What are some important lessons you and your team have learned from failure?

3) As you look back on your last few hires, would you say you hired too quickly, too slowly, or just right? Explain your answer.

4) How would you describe the culture of your team?

5) What are the factors that build trust?

6) What erodes it?

7) What needs to change?

8) As you consider applying for grants and having a more robust community involvement, how do you expect people on your team and in your church to respond? What are some ways you can help them get excited about the opportunities?

CHAPTER 8

GETTING GRANT-READY

For decades (centuries, really), Christian thinkers have wrestled with how we should relate to our culture. Some believe the right relationship is to have no relationship—to stand *against* culture. Others take the opposite view and believe that we need to avoid making waves, so we should *assimilate* into the culture. But a third way is to live with such grace, truth, and strength that we *transform* culture.[18] For this to happen, we need to be "in the world but not of the world," to love people, no matter who they are and what they believe, so we earn the right to tell them about the life-changing love of Jesus.

Daniel understood that this stance required wisdom and courage. He came on the scene at one of the most tragic moments in the history of God's people. The fierce Babylonians had invaded Judah, destroyed the beautiful and holy temple, killed many, and hauled others off to exile. In the

---

18 Richard H. Niebuhr, *Christ and Culture* (New York: Harper & Row, 1975).

pagan city, many of the Jews lost hope. They were devastated by the death and destruction in their homeland—it appeared God had abandoned them. King Nebuchadnezzar ordered his chief of staff to bring the finest young men from Judah to be trained to serve him. Among those chosen, he found four outstanding men; one of them was Daniel.

The king provided a ten-day banquet of the finest food in the land, but the four Jews asked to eat only vegetables and drink water so they could remain true to their spiritual commitments. At the end of this time, the four were the healthiest of them all. Then they were brought before the king.

> *When the training period ordered by the king was completed, the chief of staff brought all the young men to King Nebuchadnezzar. The king talked with them, and no one impressed him as much as Daniel, Hananiah, Mishael, and Azariah. So, they entered the royal service. Whenever the king consulted them in any matter requiring wisdom and balanced judgment, he found them ten times more capable than any of the magicians and enchanters in his entire kingdom.—Daniel 1:18-20*

They were *in* the center of Babylonian power, but they remained faithful to God—they were not *of* Babylonian power. The four men were tested again and again, and each time, they trusted God to deliver them . . . even from the heat of a furnace that killed those who threw them in! They were deeply connected to the power center of Babylon, but they were even more deeply connected to God.

It's important that we, as Christian leaders, live in a way that impresses the people in authority in our cities. Talk is cheap; intentions aren't enough. They need to see us in action as we faithfully and creatively serve people. The historian who wrote about the kings of Israel and Judah described the encounter between the Queen of Sheba and King Solomon. She lived hundreds of miles away, but she heard stories of his wisdom and power, so she decided to take a look for herself. She arrived in Jerusalem with "a great caravan of camels loaded with spices, large quantities of gold, and precious jewels" (1 Kings 10:2), and she asked him a lot of questions. But their dialogue wasn't the only thing that impressed her. The historian explains:

Solomon had answers for all her questions; nothing was too hard for the king to explain to her. When the queen of Sheba realized how very wise Solomon was, and when she saw the palace he had built, she was overwhelmed. She was also amazed at the food on his tables, the organization of his officials and their splendid clothing, the cup-bearers, and the burnt offerings Solomon made at the Temple of the Lord. She exclaimed to the king, "Everything I heard in my country about your achievements and wisdom is true! I didn't believe what was said until I arrived here and saw it with my own eyes. In fact, I had not heard the half of it! Your wisdom and prosperity are far beyond what I was told. How happy your people must be! What a privilege for your officials to stand here day after day, listening to your wisdom!

Praise the Lord your God, who delights in you and has placed you on the throne of Israel. Because of the Lord's eternal love for Israel, he has made you king so you can rule with justice and righteousness."—vv. 3-9

What do the stories from the Bible about Daniel and Solomon have to do with getting ready to pursue grants from government and other funding agencies? Everything! We need to be like Daniel and his friends, living with a kingdom of God mindset as we serve in the kingdom of this world. Like them, we interact with the power structures with wisdom and tact, but we never abandon our commitment to Christ and His gospel. And like Solomon, we welcome outsiders to see what we're doing. The Queen of Sheba wasn't just impressed and rode away on her camels. She invested in what Solomon was doing: "Then she gave the king a gift of 9,000 pounds of gold, great quantities of spices, and precious jewels. Never again were so many spices brought in as those the queen of Sheba gave to King Solomon" (v. 10). Today's value of just the 9,000 pounds of gold would be over $218 million!

Excellence—in compassion and care—becomes a magnet for additional resources.

Solomon didn't need her gifts. His kingdom was already incredibly wealthy. In the same way, when people see the depth of our love and the excellence of our programs, they sometimes give us resources we didn't ask for and don't really need. Excellence—in compassion and care—becomes a magnet for additional resources. Sometimes we find ways to use them, and sometimes we pass them along to others. Agency executives notice when organizations over-promise and under-deliver; we're committed to under-promise and over-deliver. It matters.

BEFORE FUNDING

As proposals are being written, we need to be confident we can live up to the described commitments. If a church or nonprofit isn't sure it can perform with excellence, the leaders need to take a step back to consider the nature and scope of the proposal. For example, executing a grant-funded program in a church setting requires a blend of faithfulness and excellence. Balancing these aspects involves being true to the organization's mission and values while effectively managing the program to meet or exceed the expectations of both the grantor and the community. Sloppy execution results in a black mark for the church (and the Church) with the funding agency and, by reputation, with other agencies in the future.

We believe that some comments like, "We tried that, and it didn't work," weren't spoken because the funding source was difficult to work with but because the leaders weren't adequately prepared so they could perform the program at a high level.

We may want to be known as "people of great faith," but that's not the way to write grant proposals. We need to also be "people of genuine reality," carefully considering the limits of what we can do. We've talked with leaders who had a bold vision to create a program, but they wrote the proposal with promises to provide resources they had no idea they could find. They insisted, "God will provide!" That's not a recipe for a positive, long-term relationship with a Funder. They want to know that God has already provided the manpower, facilities, and other resources . . . before they write the check.

Organizations work well with funding agencies when the program aligns with the organization's core beliefs, mission, and vision. The program should reflect the ethos of the organization or church as it serves the community. For example, if your church is noted for its music, proposing an after-school program to teach kids to play instruments and sing is a perfect fit, but if your church doesn't even have a piano, you need to think of another kind of outreach. But if an agency requires a curriculum that violates the church's beliefs, even though it offers an opportunity to connect with unreached people, leaders need to look for better alignment.

At one point, we had a chance to partner with another organization and receive sizable grant funding, but the other organization didn't have Christian roots. We made it clear from the outset that our staff members would pray, we'd look for opportunities to talk to people about Jesus after the program finished each day, and we were committed to representing Jesus in everything we do. We explained that we weren't using our faith as an excuse for shoddy efforts, and in fact, our faith inspires us to go above and beyond the stated requirements.

WHEN THE MONEY COMES

When the grant is awarded, it's not the time to become faithful and excellent. We may want to be judged by our intentions, but that's not how life works. If you haven't demonstrated faithfulness and excellence before, you're not going to demonstrate them now. It doesn't work to assign the implementation of a new community-based program to someone who is inexperienced or is already smothered with responsibilities. If it's a priority to connect with people in the community, you may need to rearrange job descriptions so the people involved have enough time, energy, and emotional bandwidth to do an excellent job.

Of course, we believe God for great things as the program is implemented, and we believe God will provide more manpower and resources to expand the programs. Through it all, this is a deeply spiritual enterprise: We seek God's guidance at every step, sensing His leading, asking for clarity and direction, trusting Him to provide all the necessary resources, and asking Him to use everything we do to change lives and honor Him.

Each person has particular talents, experiences, and gifts. Our team functions well because each of us brings something different to the table. Patrick Lencioni observes "The Six Types of Working Genius in a Fulfilled and Engaged Team." These are very different from one another, but identifying each person's genius propels affirmation and collaboration. The types are:

> ➤ Wonder—These are visionaries who see potential in an idea.

- Invention—They are an engine of new ideas.
- Discernment—They accurately assess people and possibilities.
- Galvanizing—They encourage others to take action.
- Enablement—They bring new ideas to life.
- Tenacity—They don't quit until the project is completed.[19]

For instance, I (Tony) am the visionary, Dianna is the detail person, and Keisha has the engineering mind to construct every element of the program and proposal. This effort isn't all we do, but it's an important part of what we do. God has called us to reach our "Jerusalem, throughout Judea, in Samaria, and to the ends of the earth" (Acts 1:8). Our church is Jerusalem, our neighborhood is Judea, the next neighborhoods are Samaria, and our efforts in other parts of the country and the world are at "the ends of the earth."

No one forces you to do something you don't want to do. You had the vision, you wrote the proposal, and you have the authority to make it happen according to your plan.

---

19 Patrick Lencioni, "The Six Types of Working Genius," https://www.thegrowthfaculty.com/blog/6typesofworkinggenius.

Quite often, the time between the approval of funding and the launch of the program is short. For example, one of our clients received a grant approval on October 12, and the agency expected implementation to begin three days later. If we hadn't helped them prepare so they had everything in place before they submitted the grant request, they couldn't have done it. Thankfully, such a quick turnaround is an exception. It's far more common to receive the green light for an approved grant proposal in May or June with a start date in August. This provides about three months to hire our staff, recruit clients, secure program resources, and be ready to go.

Remember: this is your organization's plan and program. No one forces you to do something you don't want to do. You had the vision, you wrote the proposal, and you have the authority to make it happen according to your plan.

We've heard stories of organizations that used grant funds in ways that were very different from the purposes and strategies described in their proposals or failed to abide by the guidelines in the contract. One time, it wasn't them . . . it was us. We were guilty of cutting corners. One of our earliest proposals submitted to The Children's Trust was to provide money for "Hip Arts," a creative after-school program for middle school students to teach them hip-hop dance moves, songwriting (lyricism), graphic design (tagging), life skills, and the finer points of being a DJ. Any organization that works with young people must complete Level 2 background checks for their employees—<u>Before</u> they start working. We were in a time crunch. We recruited a man who had impeccable credentials and the right experience. He was, we were sure, an

A1 hire. We had him go through the screening process, but before we got the green light, we put him on the job. A couple of weeks later, we got his results back, and to our shock, he wasn't cleared to work. We had violated our contract, and it was a mess all around. We had to tell him that he couldn't work for us, and since his work wasn't covered by the grant, we had to repay the agency for the money paid to him. But the damage was worse than that. We'd broken trust with the funding agency, and they declined to renew our contract. An agency official told us, "We consider this breach a big red flag." We didn't do what we committed to do, but we learned a valuable lesson: Don't cut corners . . . don't try to fudge the system. Our reputation was tarnished, and we paid a high price in eroded trust. It's hard to build trust, and it's much harder to rebuild it.

MANAGING THE PROGRAM

We've already described the importance of doing what we say we'll do. Integrity needs to be a thread that runs through everything, from start to finish. Following timelines and submitting reports aren't the most exciting parts of running effective programs that change lives, but they're required by every funding agency. This is part of the price we pay to plan and execute life-changing programs in our community.

Transparency is important. If the agency discovers that an organization has sugar-coated some difficulties, trust takes a couple of steps backward. The future of the relationship is at stake, so be honest about any setbacks. In most cases, the people at the funding agencies are very understanding and give plenty of grace, even if they aren't believers. They know what it's like to launch and manage a program so they're not surprised when organizations run into roadblocks. Quite often, they've seen these difficulties before, so they have creative suggestions about overcoming them.

THE PROCESS

If you want to learn to play the piano, you're not surprised if you hit the wrong keys pretty often for the first months of practice. If you want to try your hand at tennis, you'll probably need to watch some instructional videos and find someone patient enough to show you how to place your feet and extend your backswing. And if you want to learn a new language, you begin with the simplest phrases and gradually add more vocabulary and complexity to your sentences. It's the same pattern with getting grant-ready and following through to produce excellent programs for your community. If you haven't done it before, the first steps seem odd, awkward, and uncertain, but after you practice for a while, the process becomes second nature.

How do you learn to write a winning grant proposal? By looking at samples, writing your own, and getting feedback from people who have done it many times before. How do you gather the resources to pull off the program? By learning from past mistakes so you're prepared, even the first time, and even better prepared for all the ones that follow. How can you identify the right people for the community program team? By seeing them in action for months, if not years, finding out what captures their hearts, and gathering the right team together.

Over the past almost twenty years, we've had our ear to the ground to identify the needs in our community. We have a large network of contacts in churches, nonprofits, city government, and agencies who want to have a profound impact on the city, and they are very sensitive to these needs. We've learned a lot from them. We also have relationships with officials at a number of agencies. If the need, the agency resources, and the fit with our vision and capacity are compatible, we apply for the grant, prepare the resources, implement the program, and watch God work. I (Dianna) looked over our history of writing grant proposals to see our success rate. I couldn't remember ever being turned down, but I wanted to be sure. I was right: We've never been turned down, and we have far more opportunities now than we've ever had because agencies trust us. All praise to God!

When we started, we learned by trial and error. Now, we're seasoned veterans, and we consult with church and nonprofit leaders so they can learn from our experience and move more smoothly and quickly into effective programs. We help organizations get grant-ready, restructure their organizational charts to have the right people in the right roles, match their vision with potential funding agencies, write their first proposals to articulate their vision and program, launch their program, and manage it well.

Many people give the piano, tennis, or a new language a brief try, but it takes more work than they first envisioned, so they find reasons to quit. We understand. Investing time

and heart in these pursuits may take more than they bar-
gained for, but when they stop, they miss out on the payoff of
playing beautiful music, the joy of playing a sport relatively
well and having real conversations with people who speak
other languages. Each person has to calculate: Is the payoff
worth the effort?

We've met with leadership teams for a day, and when we
were done, we answered their pressing questions and helped
them make some decisions to get grant-ready. After that, they
were off and running! But we've also met with teams and
walked away with a different conclusion. Sometimes, they
didn't have the people they needed for the team, or the lead
pastor wasn't quite on board yet, or their decision-making
process hadn't been honed, so adding a new set of decisions,
a new team within the team, and orchestrating new resources
for the task was simply too high a bar for them. We explained
that we could help them get ready, but we were honest about
their deficiencies and explained how to fill in the holes. If the
pastor or nonprofit leader is the sole decision maker, the team
isn't ideally set up for community outreach. Collaboration is
the key to running these programs, so the decision-making
process has to be pushed down to other team members.

Teams don't need everything to be perfect in order to move
forward with the vision of using grants to fund outreaches in
the community, but they need good enough leadership, good
enough planning, good enough existing resources, and good
enough chemistry so they can address problems without
running the car into a ditch.

BURIED IN THE GROUND

Some people might assume that using grant funds for outreach programs is only for small churches or organizations that have few resources or for organizations in marginalized parts of a city where offerings are sparse. We believe this view is woefully limited. The right questions are from a different angle: How big is your vision? Does it extend beyond the walls of your organization or church? Does it reach out to people who don't take the initiative to come to you? If you want to go into your Samaria, where people need to see the compassion of Jesus lived out by people in your organization or church, you will need more money to care for them. Where will you get it? Grants are low-hanging fruit.

I (Tony) have seen large churches with big budgets raise money from agencies to fund programs that are far outside the perimeter of their church property. They're not being greedy. Not in the least. They're just using every possible resource to expand God's forever kingdom. Can small organizations pull this off? Yes, I can assure you it's possible because we did it, and we were about as small as it gets! The issue isn't size; it's heart, vision, and persistence.

Matthew records Jesus speaking several parables shortly before His last meal with the disciples. One of the parables was about a wealthy man who went on a trip and left his possessions in the care of three servants. The one who was entrusted with five bags of silver invested the money and earned five more. The one who was given two bags earned two more. But the servant who was given one bag hid the money in the ground. When the man came home, he asked his servants to give an accounting. He was full of praise for the first two, but he was harshly critical of the one who had buried his money. The man told him, "You wicked and lazy servant! If you knew I harvested crops I didn't plant and gathered crops I didn't cultivate, why didn't you deposit my money in the bank? At least I could have gotten some interest on it" (Matthew 25:26-27). Then he gave this instruction:

> Take the money from this servant, and give it to the one with the ten bags of silver. To those who use well what they are given, even more will be given, and they will have an abundance. But from those who do nothing, even what little they have will be taken away. —vv. 28-29

The servant with ten bags had proven to be diligent and faithful, and he received even more than the proceeds from his investments. Jesus' point is crystal clear: Be like the servant who invested his resources and multiplied what was given to him, and don't be like the "wicked and lazy" servant who did too little with what the owner put into his hands.

When we have a scarcity mentality, we're satisfied with these tokens, but when God gives us a wider, deeper, longer vision to make a difference, we find ways to do more.

If we look around, we'll see there are far more resources for outreach than we ever imagined. Most church leaders are leaving a lot of money buried in the ground . . . money they could invest to touch the lives of people who would never take the first step to come to church on their own. Many organizations and churches have some outreach efforts to serve local nonprofit organizations. That's a good first step, but they could do much more. For some, these efforts are tokens. They aren't deep, sustained connections with people in need. When we have a scarcity mentality, we're satisfied with these tokens, but when God gives us a wider, deeper, longer vision to make a difference, we find ways to do more.

Most pastors we know are already redlining with more to do than time to do it. They feel the pressure to prepare their messages, visit the sick, care for the elderly, lead their teams, keep the organization rolling, and, oh yeah, handle the conflicts, large and small, that seem to consume their time and attention. We're not blind to these stresses. We're only asking leaders to remember their calling and restructure their roles to be more effective in earning the trust of people in their communities. We believe vision attracts leadership, and God will bring gifted people to share the vision—and the burden—of this vital ministry.

When we arrived in Miami and opened Citi Church, we didn't have the luxury of sitting back and watching people stream through our doors. They were suspicious of us, so we had to take the initiative and serve them before they would trust us enough to come to church. We had no other choice but to launch outreach programs. Other churches are in communities where there are plenty of Christians who will show up, so the leaders don't have a desperate need to go "to the highways and byways to invite" people to come to the banquet of God's magnificent grace. But God is desperate for those people to trust in Him. We believe He is calling all of us to do more to reach people who won't come to church and to reach them, we need to serve them first. That's what this is all about. Will this require adjustments? Certainly. Will some job descriptions need to change? Undoubtedly. Will churches need more sources of funding? You bet. Will you do what it takes to reach more people?

THINK ABOUT IT:

1) Describe the different mindsets of church leaders who are fiercely against the culture, those who have assimilated into the culture, and those who seek to transform the culture with the love and power of Christ.

2) Which one best represents your perspective? Explain your answer.

3) What are some lessons we learn from Daniel's career in Nebuchadnezzar's court and the Queen of Sheba's visit with Solomon?

4) What are some concrete steps to become grant-ready before you submit your proposal?

5) What do you need to know, be, and do as soon as the proposal is approved for funding?

6) What principles of learning to play a musical instrument, becoming proficient at a new sport, and learning a new language apply to the learning curve associated with grant-funded community outreach?

7) Do you believe there are some resources "buried in the ground" that you could use to touch the lives of people who have never come to your church? If so, what are they?

CHAPTER 9

NUTS AND BOLTS

When I (Keisha) studied electrical engineering at Clemson University, I entered a world of discovery. I was already interested in the subject, of course, but even in my first classes, we dove into the details of how to design, create, and test all kinds of electrical equipment . . . and later, we learned how to design these things so they could be mass-produced without losing structural integrity. Some of the classes were theoretical, teaching us high-level concepts, but I especially enjoyed the hands-on coursework, designing and putting together such varied instruments as electric motors, navigation systems, and communication networks. When I joined Pastor Tony and Pastor Dianna, I assumed my education had been a waste, but I soon discovered I was wrong. I could apply the methods I'd learned in engineering to writing effective grant proposals.

I (Tony) certainly don't have the engineering background Keisha has, but I've learned to be observant and determined to accomplish new goals. Recently, I ordered a kit to build a universal gym. When I opened the box, I saw that it had about 800 parts—framing, bolts, screws, wires, and weights (among other things I can't name). I put everything out on the floor so I knew where to find each part, and I waded through the instruction book page by page. A YouTube video let me see what each step looked like. It took me two days, but in the end, it wasn't dangerous (that was my basic goal). In fact, it works really well! I'd never built a universal gym before, but now I can show others how to do it.

Throughout my childhood, I (Dianna) always imagined going into business. It seemed like the good, right, and logical thing to do. My mother's family farmed and owned businesses, so I assumed it was in my blood. I daydreamed about leading a large company with a lot of teams, doing great work, and making a lot of money. When I was eight, my mother baked chocolate chip cookies and sour cream cookies so my siblings and I could take them in a wagon from house to house in our neighborhood. We sold a baker's dozen for a dollar. I was sure I was on my way to business success!

My parents were missionaries in South Florida, so we didn't have much money. They wanted to take the family to Disney World, but it was far too expensive (even back then). Our part of the city had big softball tournaments on Friday nights, and people drank a lot of beer. On Saturday mornings, my siblings and I went to the fields and filled big trash bags with cans. We took them to the aluminum recycling center and sold them by the pound. After a few months, we made enough money for our whole family to go to Disney World.

Money isn't a mystery to me, and I'm not afraid to look for new ways to find it.

My experiences taught me to see money as an instrument of good. When I see a need and a lack of resources to meet it, I'm not surprised, and I'm not immobilized. I'm not afraid to ask people to contribute to a cause I believe in. As a missionary kid, I grew up on the generosity of people, and I have firsthand experience in seeing people give and be blessed for their giving. When they catch a vision, they're eager to fund it.

Money isn't a mystery to me, and I'm not afraid to look for new ways to find it. My past experiences prepared me for the vision God has given us to use grant funding to touch the lives of far more people than we can do without it.

Many people hear about the possibility of funding community-based programs using government grants, and they only see it from 30,000 feet. From that vantage point, it looks too complex, requiring skills and experience they don't have. They give up before they've even started. But when you look at the possibilities from street level, you can identify the specific elements. Then, fear is replaced by growing confidence as you implement specific processes and practices, and wide doors of opportunity open to you.

A couple of people have told us, "We don't need all those details. We'll just pray and trust God to soften the hearts of the officials at the agencies. Then they'll give us the money." They're right about the necessity of prayer—we certainly need to trust God for wisdom and favor, but they're wrong about the need for God to soften hearts. People who serve in these funding agencies already want to make a difference in their communities. That's why they applied for their jobs! The hurdle isn't their hearts. The hurdle is the organization's alignment with the purposes of the funding agency.

After Yvonne Sawyer encouraged us to write and submit our first grant proposal for an after-school program, we had a jumble of emotions. We were exhausted because we'd worked so hard to write it. We were hopeful we'd get the money so we could make inroads with students and their families, but we were afraid we'd missed something that would short-circuit our application. Before we put it in the mail, we laid hands on it and asked God to bless our effort. Every day, we waited (impatiently) for the response. Would we hear today? Have they had long enough to make a decision? When we got the approval, we were overjoyed and amazed at this new open door . . . and we quickly realized the work to build trust and relationships with people around us was just beginning.

By the tenth grant proposal we submitted, we had more confidence in ourselves and the process. We had very little anxiety but a lot of hope. Today, we still pray at every stage of the process—to discern the needs in the community, to find out what other nonprofits are doing to meet those needs, to identify the agencies that might fund our program, to design the program so it aligns with our values and the values of the funding agency, to write and submit the proposal, and for favor among those making the decision. Our experience is priceless, but we don't take anything for granted. We're deeply dependent on the Spirit of God to work in us, in the people at the funding agency, and in the lives of those we serve. God is at the center of every step we take. We pray, "Father, you called us to this expanded ministry in our city, and you gave us favor many times in the past. We're trusting you to give us your wisdom before, during, and after we write the proposal so lives are touched, hearts are won, and your kingdom expands. We can't make all this happen. We can play our part, but we trust you to bring the power, compassion, and impact."

We're deeply dependent on the Spirit of God to work in us, in the people at the funding agency, and in the lives of those we serve.

Just a few days before writing this chapter, a lady who asked us for assistance was told her application was accepted and that the grant for $15,000 would fund her program. When she told us, we celebrated with her! (It's always exciting, no matter how many times it happens.) That's for the first six weeks. If she performs well, the agency may give her $50,000 next year.

The bump is already in the proposal. She has to prove herself first, and then a much wider door opens for her. Of course, we're going to help her exceed the agency's expectations so she has greater opportunities down the road. If she wants to create other programs in the future, her good reputation with one funding agency will follow her when she applies to a different one.

Here is the street view of writing winning grant proposals:

1) Preparation

> Identify specific needs in the community. Talk to leaders and ask open-ended questions. Walk around the neighborhoods to notice the struggles people face.

> Consider the kinds of programs you could implement to meet specific needs.

> Find out what nonprofits are already working—and effective—in your area.

> Research potential funding sources that fit your values and manpower, including a wide array of government agencies but also private foundations.

> Study the guidelines articulated by the funding source to be sure you meet eligibility requirements, and you understand the purpose of the agency or foundation.

2) Executive summary

> Write a brief description of the mission and vision of your organization. Don't write it like an article for a garden club—leave out the flowery language! And you're not using War and Peace as the template for the length. Keep it short and crisp.

- State the need you plan to meet or the problem you want to solve.
- Clearly describe the goals and objectives of your program.
- Identify the amount of the grant you're asking for. Many agencies have information on their websites describing the amounts they may grant.

3) Introduction
- You'll repeat much of the description of your organization you included in the executive summary, but here, you can be more thorough.
- Explain your organization's mission and history.
- Give brief bios of your leadership, especially those who will implement the program.
- List your past achievements and include some success stories.

4) Statement of the need
- Provide a detailed description of the need you plan to meet.
- Include research, especially about the local area, that supports your observation of the problem.
- Write anecdotes and stories that have an emotional tug.

5) Goals and objectives
- Identify the goal and the result your program is designed to achieve.
- Outline the objectives with specific, measurable steps to meet the goal.

6) Methodology/approach

➤ Write a detailed plan to achieve your goals and objectives.

➤ Identify the leader(s) of the effort.

➤ Note any other organizations that will collaborate with you.

➤ List any experts who will provide assistance.

➤ Include a timeline for launch, continuation, and completion.

7) Evaluation

➤ Describe how you will measure the success of your program, including instruments, metrics, and methods to collect accurate data.

➤ Identify the reporting structure and timeline.

8) Sustainability

➤ Write a plan for the program's future after the grant period ends.

➤ Identify any other potential sources of funding.

➤ Describe your long-term vision for the program's impact.

9) Budget

➤ Create a detailed budget for the money provided by the agency or foundation.

➤ Include categories of salaries, equipment, curriculum, travel, overhead, etc.

➤ Justify the rationale for each item in the budget.

10) Conclusion

➤ Summarize the proposal: the need, the goal and objectives, and the anticipated impact of the program.

> Express gratitude for the agency or foundation's consideration.

11) Appendices (if necessary)

> Include any important supporting documents, including letters from leaders in the community, resumes of key personnel, brochures describing your organization, and further research.

12) Proofreading and review

> Use Grammarly or another word-processing tool to correct any errors.

> Confirm the program's alignment with the grantor's requirements.

> If possible, have someone with experience in grant writing review the document and give feedback.

13) Submission

> Meticulously follow the submission guidelines. (You don't want to create resistance from the beginning!)

> If the proposal is submitted electronically, be sure your document is compliant with the required file size and format. Also, be sure to comply with all word count and character limits.

> If the proposal is provided as a hard copy, be sure it's on high-quality paper and the printing is sharp.

14) Post-submission

> If the proposal is approved, the next phase is contracting to finalize all the elements of funding and implementation.

> Those who receive funding are expected to comply with all administrative and reporting requirements.

> ❯ If the grant request is denied, ask for feedback so you can do better next time.
> ❯ Most grant funders have an appeal process, so if there was something missing, you may have an opportunity to appeal the decision and still get funded.

Remember that grant writing is both an art and a science. Tailor each proposal to the specific agency or foundation and make your case compelling both rationally and emotionally.

(After the last chapter, you'll find information about using us, at 305 Unlimited, to consult with you and your organizations to smooth the process of applying for grant funding and designing effective programs.)

SAMPLE GRANT PROPOSAL

If you would like to see a sample of one our winning proposals, you can use this QR code to access one on our website. Of course, the details need to be tailored to the needs of your community, the particular program you want to have, and other details to be sure your organization and the agency are in alignment.

THINK ABOUT IT:

1) When was the last time you built something from a kit?

2) How did it go?

3) What did you learn about yourself from the process?

4) Review the components of a grant proposal. Which elements seem simple and easy?

5) Which ones are more daunting? Explain your answer.

6) Who on your team or in your organization would be a good fit to work on a grant proposal?

7) What are your observations about the sample grant application?

8) What do you need to take the first step?

CHAPTER 10

IT'S WORTH IT!

Pastor Lonnie Johns at Christ Central Church in Lake City, Florida, heard what we're doing in Miami and asked for our help. We coached him and his team to identify a need they could meet in their community and find government agencies that could help them meet the need. They wanted to launch a school, which required a lot of work on a curriculum, administrators, teachers, other staff members, facilities, students, and a timeline. We walked with them, providing coaching and insight along the way for each compliance item as they applied to the Florida Department of Education to start a private Christian school. Because of our experience of walking through this process, we were able to clarify any questions, make recommendations, and provide resources and feedback during the application process.

Pastor Lonnie and his team were overjoyed when their school application was approved, and so were we! All the pieces fit well. They had done their homework and were starting a school aligned with the values of the church. They opened the school with ninety-five students in their first year. Pastor Lonnie told us they could have easily had more students, but they wanted to make sure they did it right from the beginning. They plan to add more grades next year, with probably 200 students. Pastor Lonnie and his team have a beautiful blend of humility and boldness. They knew what they didn't know. So, they asked for help, and when they got the help they needed, they launched a terrific new school, Kingdom Culture Academy, in Lake City, Florida.

We've talked with church leaders who don't quite grasp the nature of grant funding. They assume their budget will take a hit even if they get grant money. Yes, they almost certainly need to invest some time and money at the beginning to write the first proposal, but the long-term benefits (monetary and non-monetary) of grants usually outweigh any initial investment of capital or resources. And some programs, like church-sponsored private schools, can have a net surplus that goes to the church's general fund. So, before you make a misguided assumption, do your homework to adjust your expectations . . . or give us a call or visit our website.

The opportunities are enormous. In only a few years, we've created a wide range of programs in our part of Miami, touching the lives of students and their families, leading countless people to Christ, and growing our church from ten people to a thriving congregation. Our community outreach programs have received over $20 million in grants. With our experience, we're helping nonprofits and churches in other cities and states do what we've done. In 2023, our clients have been awarded over $6 million dollars of funding.

Like any learning curve, the first part is steep, but we also see the principle of the flywheel: The same amount of effort required to start it turning generates much more speed as the flywheel accelerates. In other words, efficiencies increase with experience.

The source of the money is simply a resource to enable you to have a bigger impact.

Sports teams have coaches, and rising professionals have mentors. In any new venture, it's crucial to have someone who can help you anticipate opportunities and challenges, structure your resources for maximum effect, encourage you to take the next step, and celebrate every success. Yvonne Sawyer was our coach, and she was instrumental in our success. She gave us the idea and the vision, and she patiently walked with us through the early stages. Along the way, she has remained a valued resource. Sometimes, when we were unsure about a decision, a five-minute phone call with her gives us all the information we need. On that day when we meet Jesus and He makes all things right, Yvonne will receive a prophet's reward.

If your heart has been moved by our stories, find someone to help you have a far greater impact in your community than ever before. That's the point: It's not about the money;

it's about the impact. The source of the money is simply a resource to enable you to have a bigger impact.

In his letter to the Romans, Paul assured them that with God, "there is no respect of persons" (Romans 2:11, KJV). Throughout the centuries, God has used unlikely people to do great things for His kingdom. Abraham lied twice about his wife Sarah, Jacob was a deceiver, Moses vacillated between courage and cowardice, Peter was impulsive, Paul was a hitman, and the story of the church is a litany of men and women who, by the calling of God and the power of the Spirit, were transformed and then changed communities and cultures. In fact, God seems to delight in using misfits and outcasts to accomplish His purposes—the three of us belong in that category. When we arrived in Miami, we had a dream of planting a God-honoring church, but we crashed into the stark reality that the people in our part of the city wouldn't trust us. We were desperate to find a way to connect with them, and the Lord led us to Yvonne. We knew nothing about finding grants to fund programs to reach our community, and in fact, we knew less than nothing because we believed many of the myths we listed in Chapter 2. But we realized this was an opportunity God had put in our laps, so we devoted ourselves to trusting God to make it work.

Has it been difficult at times? Yes. Have we needed to do more work to align our vision with the purposes of agencies? Certainly. But has it been worth it? Oh, yes! When we see a family we met through tutoring their child show up at church, we see the hand of God at work. When we notice a smile from a kid whose life has been a series of heartaches, we know we're on the right track. When we have favor from the mayor and city council to open doors we didn't even know existed, we're humbled by God's amazing grace. When we see a couple whose marriage was on the brink because of alcohol, drugs, and abuse, and now they hold hands when they walk into our services, we give glory to God. When we look at the faces of people in our congregation on Sunday morning and see a sea of people whose first contact with us was through outreach programs, we're amazed that God would use such creative ways to draw people to Himself. The vision God gave me (Tony) when I first stepped into the building has become a reality. All praise to God!

It's worth everything we've invested in this vision . . . and so much more.

> **When our hearts are both melted and molded by the enormity of the grace God has lavished on us, we look for ways to pay it forward.**

Jesus stepped out of heaven to become a helpless child, and on the cross, He took the judgment we deserve so we could receive the honor and welcome He deserves. As a response to this immense wealth of love, it only makes sense to follow

Him by reaching out to connect with the people He loves. Paul's letter to the Philippians was a thank-you note for their involvement and support of his ministry. After his beautiful poem (maybe a song in the early church) about the love, humility, and power of Christ, he explains what difference Christ's sacrifice made in his life: "But even if I am being poured out like a drink offering on the sacrifice and service coming from your faith, I am glad and rejoice with all of you. So you too should be glad and rejoice with me" (Philippians 2:17-18, NIV). It is our unspeakable privilege to be poured out for those we love and serve.

When our hearts are both melted and molded by the enormity of the grace God has lavished on us, we look for ways to pay it forward. Community impact is one way, and it's a good one. It begins with curiosity ("Can this happen in my organization, my church and my community?"), becomes a continually clarifying vision ("I can see this kind of program working very well here!"), and soon becomes research, planning, and writing the first grant proposal. Then, when leaders see the kind of impact in their communities that we've seen at Citi Church, the momentum becomes unstoppable.

Let us give you a few more snapshots of changed lives:

> Luis and Nestor Bussi's parents came to America from the Dominican Republic. When we met them, Nestor was in kindergarten, and Luis was several years older. Like most immigrants, their parents were strapped for money. Their mom, Maria, began working at a local daycare, and it was very difficult for her to pick up the kids after school. Our after-school program was a lifeline

for her and her family. The children stayed in our programs all through elementary, junior high, and high school years. Luis joined the military and was trained as a mechanic. He now services high-end cars. Nestor went to college and then medical school. Today, Maria still works at the same daycare, and she cooks full Latin meals for my (Keisha) kids, Legacy and Legend, every day. It's amazing how God works! We served her children, and now she serves mine.

➤ One student was a sensitive and deeply troubled boy. His mother stayed high on cocaine and heroin, and his dad was out of the picture. He basically raised himself. We welcomed him to our school, and we poured love and security into him. Still, his anger sometimes got the best of him. He would explode or rebel, but soon, he came back with a heart of repentance. We weren't surprised that kids from backgrounds like his feel terribly unsafe and act out in different ways, but his tender heart made him easy to love. When he was a freshman on our school's baseball team, and we took the bus to play at a school outside the city, he leaned over to me and said, "Pastor Tony, this is the first time I've ever been out of Miami." He graduated from our high school and earned a scholarship to play baseball in college. His future is bright.

➤ And speaking of sports, most of the children in our school come from countries that play soccer. They've never played football, so holding a ball and carrying it was foreign to them. Our coach at the time taught them the basics of the game, and they were fast learners.

Believe it or not, our team won the Private School State Football Championship!

➤ One of the ladies in our church, Jennifer Coronel, had a dream of using a culinary program as an outreach to teenagers in the community. The idea was to provide facilities and professional chefs to teach kids how to cook. We realized this effort could attract teens who weren't involved in our other programs, so we wanted to do it, but there was a problem: The due date for proposals was just a week after she told us about it. We worked like crazy to do the research and write the proposal. We found a fully resourced commercial kitchen in the building of the local Police Benevolence Association. We were accepted, and it has been successful for many years. It's been amazing to look through the door to watch the chefs and the kids. Many of our students ate broccoli for the first time, and they learned to cook healthy, nutritious, delicious meals. The kids and the chefs met four afternoons a week. As a test of their skills (and a way to connect with more people), we invited neighbors to "Restaurant Nights," and we catered events in the city. We set up opportunities for the participants to meet with chefs in some of the finest restaurants in Miami. Today, many of our former students are working in kitchens throughout the city or serving in another capacity in the hospitality industry. Our program taught them the hard skills of learning to cook as well as the soft skills of relating to people up and down the organizational chart.

One day I (Tony) received a call from someone at City Hall. I wasn't sure what to make of the call since it was out of the blue. I was told that we were invited to a ceremony celebrating our contribution to the city of Miami. At the presentation, the mayor gave us a plaque showing the city's appreciation. I thought, Wow. We've come a long way since that depressing day when we had only ten people at our church! Now, the city has validated our impact on the people of our community! They see what kind of difference we're making.

Since then, we've received other awards. The accolades aren't very important in themselves, but they speak volumes about the reputation God has given us. We've become valued partners with city leaders. What an honor, what a privilege, what a responsibility!

Another name for Jesus is Emmanuel, which means "God with us." Jesus came to be with us, to share His life with us, and to impart His love and power to us. Citi Church has the same mission: We want the people of Miami to know we're part of them, we share their joys and struggles, and we're thrilled to impart God's grace, love, strength, and purpose to the people He loves so dearly.

Will you join us? Yes, you're already doing great work for the kingdom, but it's possible to do more, much more, outside the walls of your church or organization.

THINK ABOUT IT:

1) If you've read this far in the book, you undoubtedly have a heart for the lost and the least in your community. How has God stirred you as you've read our stories and learned about our processes and practices?

2) Which of the programs we've implemented seem like low-hanging fruit for your church or organization? What difference would it make for them to be fully functioning?

3) What's your first step (or next step)? What information and resources do you need? Where will you find them?

WE CAN HELP!

Do you need some encouragement and some practical help in getting started in the world of grant funding? We can help you transform faith into funding.

At 305 Unlimited LLC, we provide specialized grant consulting services tailored just for organizations like yours. We know the word 'grant' can sound daunting—images of complicated forms, strict guidelines, and sleepless nights. If the intricacies of grants have previously felt like a maze, consider us your trusted guide to navigate and conquer it.

Why collaborate with us?

Simplified Process: We've demystified the grant process, breaking it down into manageable steps, ensuring you're never overwhelmed.

Strategic Insight: It's not just about finding grants; it's about identifying the RIGHT sources of funding. We teach you how to analyze, advise, and align your goals with opportunities that resonate with your vision.

Expert Guidance: With years of experience, we understand the nuances of faith-based, community-driven projects. We can help ensure you match your vision with the right opportunities.

Your Story, Front and Center: Your church or nonprofit has countless stories of hope, transformation, and divine intervention. We teach you how to weave these narratives into compelling proposals that impress funders.

Empowerment Through Education: We believe in empowering you. Our approach focuses on equipping your team with the knowledge and skills to approach grants with confidence in the future.

Why does this matter?

Because every successful grant means more resources to serve your community, expand your outreach, and touch more lives AND every potential grant becomes a stepping stone, propelling your organization's vision forward, widening your reach, and deepening your impact.

Don't let fear, intimidation, or the unknown stand in the way of blessings and potential breakthroughs. We can walk with you to transform uncertainties into actionable strategies, ensuring that your mission always finds its deserved support. Together, let's strategize, optimize, and realize the limitless funding potential of your faith-driven vision!

305 UNLIMITED

THE JOURNEY MADE EASY

p: 305-306-7233

🌐 **www.305unlimited.com**

✉️ **info@305unlimited.com**

📷 **the305unlimited**

f **the305unlimited**

THE AVAIL PODCAST

HOSTED BY VIRGIL SIERRA

AVAIL
PODCAST

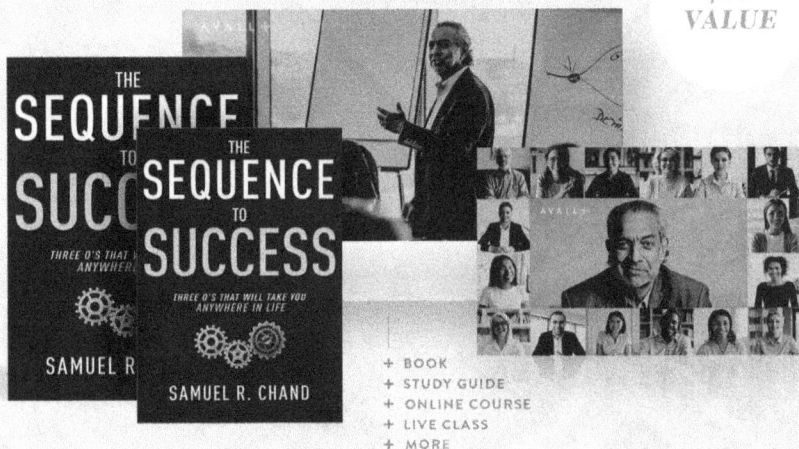

www.ingramcontent.com/pod-product-compliance
Lightning Source LLC
Chambersburg PA
CBHW070540090426
42735CB00013B/3030